AMERICAN HOAXISM

AMERICAN HOAXISM

– JEREMY STONE

AMERICAN HOAXISM

TABLE OF CONTENTS

CHAPTER ONE

AMERICAN HOAXISM

On September 11th, 2001, America and the World watched in horror as the Twin Towers were both taken down by two incredibly and unusually fast-moving commercial 747 airliners. Piloting these wieldy aircraft were pilots with such unprecedented skills in maneuvering aeronautically into low altitude and high-pressure areas at 500 miles an hour (feats of flight agility previously believed to be physically impossible) into New York City towards the Towers by Taliban terrorists trained better than any seasoned pilot in the West, having been trained in just weeks in Saudi Arabia. The precision accuracy used to fly planes into seemingly impenetrable steel-reinforced Towers, which were sliced through with ease and sophistication, had never been seen before. The world could only watch - in disbelief and wonder – hypnotized by the kind of evil this highly advanced and well-funded terrorist group could plot and carry out. One of the Radical Islamic groups involved was Al Qaeda, which reviled America, western culture, and our extravagant way of life so zealously that they were willing to take the lives of over three thousand Americans and their own lives as well. This unnecessary carnage was in the name of a Jihad or "Holy War," which was declared against the West, and to receive their promised reward in the next life – the seventy-two virgin brides, which awaited them in paradise. Seventy-two virgin brides, which could not be seen, were their only motivation for crushing the great American superpower and its 33-year-old symbol of economic power, the World Trade Center in the true capital of the United-States - New York City.

As the south towers smoke filled the air at just around 9:20, it quickly became even more apparent that this could not have been a domestic attack; it was far too sophisticated. Instead, it could only have been the work of that rich and powerful mastermind, Osama Bin Laden, the madman we've heard about so often on Television, whose violent tirades against America must now have finally been realized!

We all quietly said to ourselves that whoever is responsible for this horrific act of terror against these innocent Americans must surely pay. "Whoever they are, we must hunt these cowards down and bring them to justice." After all, these innocent victims could have been any one of us. Of course, more coordinated terrorist attacks could be looming on the horizon. "This is an act of war."

This was, of course, the official story propagandized to us by every television news outlet across America and worldwide, but was the world at large too distracted to realize they had been told a fairy-tale and yet another great American Hoax?

The truth behind 9/11 is that there are no flight records for flights 11, 77, 175, and 93 produced by American Airlines or any Commercial Airliner. Nor have any records from American Airlines or from any known Airline producing any evidence showing any passengers named by the Media were aboard any flights anywhere in the world on 9/11. All of the so-called "box-cutter terrorists" were not only nowhere in the vicinity of New York City or North America for that matter, on 9/11. Instead, the named suspects, Mohamed Atta Abdulaziz al-Omari, Satam Alsuqami, Fayez Banihamad, Marwan Alshehhi, Waleed Alshehri, Mohand Alshehri, Hamza Alghamd, Ahmed Alghamdi, Wail Alshehri, Khalid Almihdhar, Nawaf Alhazmi, Majed Moqaed, Ziad Jarrah, Ahmed Alhaznawi, Ahmed Alnami Salem, Alhazmi, and Saeed Alghamdi; suspected to be trained by al Qaeda at Afghanistan "flight schools," didn't take their lives for Allah, but were still alive, some of them still flying their regular commercial airline routes for Saudi Airlines. According to Lieutenant Stubine, "All radar in the New York area was ordered to be turned off - on that day (9/11/2001)" by Vice President Dick Cheney, who had taken shelter in the bunkered safety of the Colorado Mountains. No planes - hit the Twin Towers on 9/11, no passengers were on airplanes to hit the Twin Tower Center on 9/11, because none of the aircraft mentioned in the 9/11 Commission's Report were in existence to hit any WTC Tower on 9/11.

In this book, I'm not going to tell you what you want to hear, and I'm not going to tiptoe around the truth just to make you feel good while validating your false beliefs and perceptions about the world around you – that would be unfair to you – you deserve the truth. In this book, some of what you will learn may be extremely uncomfortable to hear since I will be essentially deprogramming you out of ignorance and into reality, one which is free from the illusions spun by the elite. Everything - we think we know about the world around us is wrong - dead wrong - and I mean everything. And - I intend to blow the lid off these hoaxed lies, which have been so deeply indoctrinated into our naive and innocent minds. The hoaxed lies fed to us by state-run media and a coordinated permeation of false history must be revealed. After reading this book and the stone-cold truths in it, you will either completely lose your mind out of weakness, or you will simply see things exactly as they are, realizing you've been fooled for the better part of your life. However, do not let yourself be ashamed of being tricked; we all have been. Instead, let yourself become empowered by the hard truths found throughout our 250-year long journey through this grand illusion of American-made lies tailor-made for American citizens and the citizens of this New World; And let this be a detailed roadmap to guide you through the ever-changing confusion tactics used in "American Hoaxism."

September 11th, 2001, from a conspiratorial standpoint, was not the first time Americans questioned Government's role in hoaxes, false flag events, psychological operations, or conspiracies designed to effect societal manipulation or the intentional plotting against American citizens. However, it was the first inside job/conspiracy which involved the direct and open mass murder of over three thousand unsuspecting and innocent Americans without cause. This was an unprecedented form of American Hoaxism. For many, it was the beginning of a universal awareness that something was very, very wrong with Government and its true intentions for American citizens. It was forming an international alliance for a totalitarian New Order.

Why are hoaxes so crucial in the creation of an American-made New World Order? We can trace hoaxes via the New World as far back as the 15th Century with Christopher Columbus's hoax foundation of America. Columbus, being an Agent of the Jesuit Order - and from there we find one American Hoax after another; from the American Revolution – yes, it was hoaxed, to 9/11, to the world's current situation. But, why? Why is America's New-World form of Government, which we call Democracy or Representative Government, so interdependent on Hoaxism? To better answer these questions about why, we must look at precisely what a hoax is, what it creates, and its effects on shaping society? Hoaxes create illusions, and these illusions very often become reality, and this false reality then becomes a societal crisis from seemingly harmless American-made hoaxes to grand illusions, to reality, to full-blown crises. This is how the World Government shapes, programs, and dominates society; through American Hoaxism. And, this is also why America's New World Order has always spun lies for its citizens from the beginning – and why it has continued to ramp up the intensity and scope of its hoaxes over half-millennium into the present day. The elite have always expressed the need for a perfect crisis - and we are now living in it; The Great scamdemic crisis – The Great Reset.

Surely, other civilizations have used hoaxes on occasion. Still, with its

New World, America is the only civilization that has capitalized on hoaxes as a way of life, forming a new culture of robotic-thinking and naively programmed people. Who believe they have some exclusive new knowledge or even "wisdom" when the only knowledge this new society has is the knowledge of ignorance, which has been imposed upon us by the lying elite and "enlightenment" thinkers who govern our minds.

The American public has been deliberately lied to about everything from its very foundation. This hoaxed world has purposefully and very deliberately been laid out by America's founding fathers to create a complete Super-Capitalist/Socialist New World Order - set to be realized by the thirty-year term between 2020 through 2050. We are now living in that predestined period of time where

America and its New World-dominated countries - which today is every country on earth - will cease to exist as we know it, and in this book, I intend to prove it beyond a shadow of a doubt. Does that mean every country on earth is secretly controlled by America, even Afghanistan, Iran, North Korea, and China? It does, and if you don't already know it, you will know it very soon – without question – the United States and its secret societies control every corner of this earth and every one of the lies built upon it. If you wish to move yourself up from ignorance, stop thinking in Republican and Democrat talking points and start thinking in reality. While Republicans, Democrats, and Libertarians are busy putting on a show for sheep, we naively fall into the trap in allowing them to group us all into camps, causing division and unnecessary strife, pitting good people one against another, all for two political agendas which seem very different on the surface, yet lead to the very same Super-Capitalist and Socialist Super-State. Their lies and hoaxes will keep you deeply indoctrinated in pure ignorance. First, I will give you some quick examples of what I mean, and then later, I will explain more about how these hoaxes work and why. Very quickly, I'll reveal two more significant but lesser-known American Hoaxes. By lesser-known, I'm telling you that you will not find this information anywhere else since it is still covered up with a mind-blowing degree of secrecy. First, we have the so-called Nuclear Hoax. The Nuclear Hoax fooled us all, that is, until now.

There are no nuclear weapons anywhere in existence anywhere on earth – not in America, not in Israel, not in North Korea. We have proof of hoaxed nuclear weapons from the fake and phony black and white 1960s footage made for propaganda and to increase fear throughout our world. "What are you saying?! Einstein, The Manhattan Project, and all the Nuclear fall-out footage were faked?" Yes, it was. And I'll tell you why- and, if you cannot accept that, go back and look at the hoaxed so-called "nuclear race" footage very carefully and examine it until the smoke clears from your brainwashed minds. You will find anomalies like all other American-made hoaxes, specifically the "in plain sight" lies.

Within the 1963 footage, you will find visuals of a barn being blasted to oblivion by what is supposed to be radioactive fallout, but notice the camera which is sitting within just 100 feet of this decimated barn and how it is never touched yet is able to capture the before and after of total annihilation. How foolish have we all been never to notice the simple things which have been right under our noses? Also, notice that the clouds behind the "mushroom cloud" never move and appear to be a cardboard cutout or a cheaply assembled Hollywood backdrop. And nuclear reactors? They are simply high-pressure steam engine power plants with an atomic company name. Chernobyl? Completely faked. People still live there, and their children do not have three eyes or any noticeable mutations; they have lived to be relatively old and are completely healthy. And WW2'S Hiroshima and Nagasaki's first use of the Atomic bomb?

Complete and utter nonsense and just more American Hoaxism for a dumbed-down and paralyzed New World. It's reported that the United States Government used tens of thousands of pounds of TNT to feign the nuclear devastation created at these Japanese World War Two sites (which were explicitly designed to target and kill off Japanese Christians, but for now, we will save that antichristian topic for another time) to affect the appearance of real atomic damage of a hoaxed nuclear explosion. But why on earth would these reasonable elite do such horrible things? It's simply to keep the world in a perpetual state of fear – as if we don't have enough in our lives, the elite believe we need more, more, and more until we are either paralyzed by fear altogether or shrink and cower before the power of these elaborate government hoaxes. Either way, we do not have to accept their lies any longer, and I promise you that once you know the truth behind these hoaxes, you will feel a sense of freedom, unlike any feeling you've had before – and it will change your life for the better. Fear is paralyzing and will make you perpetually ignorant. All history is based on perpetuating fear and the cultivation of an absolute ignorant one-world order and its resultant society, which continues to be held captive in darkness.

The second promised revelation of a worldwide hoax, also one never heard or spoken of, is the long perpetuated myth and lie that dinosaurs ever existed on this Earth, that is that Dinosaurs neither existed millions or even thousands of years ago – the existence of Dinosaurs is a complete fabrication, and yet another great American-made hoax given to us by the Darwinist movement 100 years after the theory of evolution was deliberately put forward, for the express purpose in attempting to galvanize the world with "proof" using incomplete replicas of creatures which are now found in every "dinosaur museum" in every major city in this New World. Please ask your local museum's director whether or not those bones are real, and It's guaranteed they will tell you they are all just replicas. Yes, replicas of something that doesn't exist. You can then ask the reason for this, and you'll get all sorts of insane rationale for why this is, yet the fact remains, no real dinosaur bones have ever been produced for us naïve minions to this day. Yet, somehow, we still cling to these insane elite liars for information while accepting it as gospel truth even when they give us absolutely no evidence to support their claims – their expertise and "genius" is enough for many of us to accept and trust them with our very lives - to hell with them. Dinosaurs have never existed and are one of America's most prized possessed hoaxes. The Dinosaur Hoax has been perpetuated by Corporate American hoax-for-profit moguls and its giants, namely the Rockefellers. John Rockefeller was the father of what is essentially the American side of the infamous European Rothschild family. Being born a Rothschild, Rockefeller understood America was built upon hoaxes and decided to perpetuate and cash in on his Dinosaur Hoax. Rockefeller was able to pour his big oil money into the scientific community to spread the dinosaur myth far and wide for a completely different reason. He needed adults to naively believe in these mythical creatures as children do Santa Claus; with hoaxed bones in every museum and scientific scammers working beside him, he had everything necessary to make Dinosaurs a reality for the naïve and gullible sheeple of the world. But why? John Rockefeller was a master American Hoaxer, no doubt one of the best in history since he did fool most of the world's population in the existence of something there is absolutely no proof for. He did it because he needed an excuse to make oil and petroleum appear scarce when oil is still as abundant as water (yes, please wrap your head around that for a moment), the best way for Rockefeller to actuate his goal in creating an illusion that oil was a rare and therefore a very valuable commodity was to create the illusion of extinct dinosaurs (so rare they cannot be found), which after dying produced an even rarer material known as oil. In this way, Rockefeller quickly cornered the oil industry, owning it lock, stock, and barrel within the "Scientific" community and the industrial world who were happy to back his profitable, hoaxed lie. This hoax may well be the simplest of all hoaxes, using only "scientific experts" and replica bones to fool the world. And that is how easy it was for John Rockefeller to become the newly anointed American Godfather of the hoaxed New World.

The greatest American-Made Hoaxes were all done in plain sight. The in-plain-sightness is what makes these hoaxes so convincing. For some universal and unknown psychological reason, it becomes even more difficult to see when the truth is right in front of us. To exemplify the power of in-plain-sightness, consider the mountains, and for a moment forget the theory that mountains were shaped by millions of years of continental and paleotectonic shifting, creating enormous upheavals in the structure of the earth, forming the enormous mountains we see throughout the world; Instead, look at the possibility that this convoluted yet apparently reasonable theory is nothing more than a hoaxed lie. Also, reinforce this belief by imagining just reading scientific publications stating the discovery of new advancements and scientific breakthroughs in particle and atomic sensors. These sensors can now determine that small hills and large mountains are nothing more than petrified trees and what's left of what used to be a world full of gigantically enormous trees. Wait, before scoffing at the idea, what proof do you have that shifting plates along earth explain how mountains were formed? There is no proof for this theory – this is simply an unproven theory that is now regarded as fact. However, traces of giant tree bark can be found at the base of nearly every mountain, large or small. The evidence for mountains once being gargantuan trees has a thousand times more merit than an unsupported and speculative plate tectonics theory. The following photographs are of Giant trees – excuse me – mountains, where tree bark and tree shapes can be seen in these mountains, proving that every mountain was once a tree. Now, if you find this fascinating but maybe are not entirely convinced yet, that is perfectly ok because the seed has already been planted, and you will be a believer sooner than later. The point is not whether you believe entirely in petrified mountain trees, but the possibility that most, if not all of the world's mysteries have been hidden naturally, in plain sight; and now have the added assistance of deliberate Government hoaxes and elaborate cover-ups to conceal these natural mysteries

Before delving into the second greatest hoax the world has ever known, 9/11 – the first is today's perfect world crisis. The second greatest hoax this world has ever known is that of an American Revolution, which was produced and staged by Agents of the British Government (the American Illuminati), the true masters of illusions for the shaping of a New World Order; one now filled with absolute lies, fables, and fairy tales. The American Revolution Hoax is perhaps the most elusive and fascinating hoaxes of all. This kind of hoax is rooted deeply in every one of us – especially those of us American-born citizens raised on childhood fairy tales of Paul Revere riding into town, warning, the "British are coming!", making it harder to break free from this fabricated and hoaxed illusion once and for all. I will prove the American Revolution was hoaxed - and all so-called Revolutions throughout the world have been hoaxed in every country (especially around 1776) - in the following chapter and will do so beyond a preponderance of evidence.

Many of you may already know that America was founded, not coincidentally, the same year the

Order of the Illuminati was formed; even stranger when we realize nothing significant happened on July 4th, 1776, to Constitute the definition of a revolution. The only change which took place after Independence Day was a very thin and undetailed story of an American Government overthrowing the previous British one. When we look beyond the façade of this fill-in-the-blanks and use-your-imagination sort of purposefully undetailed history, we find absolutely no change in Government taxations (because taxes remained the same), no difference in the trade between American and British goods, nor do we find any economic improvements for Americans after this phony "Revolution." In this way, America experienced the opposite of what a Revolution is by definition; it experienced its first continuity in Government by the same rulers (The

British Monarchy), only now under a different name. Moreover, the so-called 'historical proof' for any accounts concerning an American Revolution is also more than a false definition for a Revolution. It can now be proven to have been entirely faked.

Why substitute one tyrannical Government for another? The American Government, according to his-story, is supposed to be the established freedom from the tyranny of the Roman Catholic Church. However, in an interesting twist in the official narrative, the pretense of an existing schism between Roman Catholic and Freemasonry begins to fall apart quickly; Every last one of our founding fathers was both Roman Catholic, Freemasons, and Illuminatus of the Jesuit Order all simultaneously. When we're told these groups have been warring for hundred's of years, this great American Hoax of a power upheaval by Freemasons from the Roman Catholic Church also now begins to unravel, as we discover the Papal States' or Roman Catholic Church created its own arch-nemesis, the Order of Illuminati on May 1st, 1776. Yes, the Jesuit Order and the Order of the Illuminati are one and the same. They are simply two different wings on the same ancient 'Imperialist Bird.' One wing appears to fight the other.

Meanwhile, each wing washes the other, never knowing what the other is doing. To better understand this American foundational hoax, we must better understand the two most important dates in American Hoaxism, July 4th, 1776 (The hoaxed Independence Day) and May 1st,

1776 (The birth of the Illuminati), and their significance to one another. From July 4th to May 1st, 1776, there are exactly 66 days. From the 76' traditional pagan Summer solstice to the "Godly" or Roman Church's official celebration of the summer solstice, there are precisely 13 days difference – again, no coincidence in the foundation of our two-winged Imperialist bird of Hoaxism. The Pagan traditions of the Illuminati and the "Godly" traditions of the Jesuit Order were joined on July 4th, 1776, the foundation of America's separation from God and the tenants of Christianity, not the Church. The Church has always been Heretical and Anti-Christian, and the Masons knew it, being born out of the Jesuit Order. But, more on this great hoax in the following Chapter.

As we have established, hoaxes create illusions, and these illusions then create a temporary crisis, which resolves into a synthesis forming a new and false reality. But, can we call these new realities completely false? Both of these become illusions and reality in the case of 'Fiat Printed Money' and in booming economies. The perception and belief that cash has value, giving it value where none exists. The same can be said for economic booms and bullish markets; false perceptions can often produce a booming economy where none exists. Is it possible that mankind can make himself incredibly sick in simply believing in a reality that does not exist? Hoaxed Illusions shape the society of this New World; However, we do not need *their* lies to create *our* version of reality – We can and must create our own realities, built upon an even stronger foundational belief in truths. Faith in absolute truths will always win out over in a world built upon hoaxed illusions.

- *If radical Islamic terrorists were not behind the 9/11 attacks, who were the real criminals, and why did they do it?*
- *If 9/11 truly was an inside job, are the technocratic elite homicidal maniacs or just power-hungry and deluded religious fanatics?*
- *Was the concerted 9/11 hoax just another insurance scam or the beginning of creating an enhanced New World Order?*

For many, gaining an absolute and complete understanding of exactly how one of the greatest American

Hoaxes in modern times was carried out will permanently change your view of the world and only lead to more questions about where American Hoaxism ends and where reality begins.

At the point in discovering 9/11 was an inside job, most are familiar with and will predictably bring up the flight recordings and ask, "If no planes blew up the WTC Towers, then explain who the people were speaking to their loved ones on their cell phones?" This is the wrong question since cell phones were unable to get any cellular service whatsoever at 30,000 feet in 2001. Even at low elevations of say 8,000 feet, to assert it was possible to get air to ground signal from a cell phone is an extreme absurdity. According to

Qualcomm, their ability to create wireless technology which would make cellphone communication allowing airline passengers to use cell phones to interact with family onboard a commercial aircraft would be a possibility in the future – as of 2001, this technology did not exist. This technology was not a technological breakthrough – the plan was to simply equip commercial airlines with the same high-powered antennas used on the ground.

"Travelers may be talking on personal cellphones in as soon as 2006. Earlier this month [July 2004], American Airlines conducted a trial run on a modified aircraft that permitted cell phone calls."

(WPost, July 27, 2004)

This service, also known as Picco cell CDMA – with antennas built inside a plane's cabin was not a reality on 9/11/2001, making any cellular phone calls by terrorists, flight crew, or passengers on a commercial airline on 9/11 an impossibility.

'So, who made these phone calls which we heard live on State-Media verified by the 9/11 Commission?'

Here is an excerpt from the 9/11 Commission whose signal was somehow mysteriously "recorded" clear as a bell at 35,000 feet, with absolutely no break in communications: "At 8:45, the flight reaches a cruising altitude of 35,000 feet."

"Is this it? Should we finish it off?"

"Not yet. When they come - we finish will it off."

"In the cockpit. If we don't - we'll die!"

"Roll it!"

"Allah is the greatest!

Allah is the greatest!"

"Is this it? I mean - should we put it down?"

"Yes - put it in it - and pull it down."

"Pull it down! Pull it down!"

"Allah is the greatest - Allah is the greatest."

Not only is the dialogue here impossible due to the limitations in cellphone/sky phone technology, but the script is overdramatic, and leaving us with the emotional impact from a predictive programming climatic scene out of "Air Force One." The voices heard in these recordings were the voices of MOSSAD Agents and I.S.I.S. (Israeli Secret Intelligence

Services) performing their roles as 'Islamic Terrorists' working as crisis actors. After 9/11, the Israeli Government transformed American Government into a permanent Military Industrial Complex, utterly controlling and shaping U.S. foreign policy in the Middle East and abroad, using the illusion of a terrorized Israeli Nation as its manufactured 'Biblical' rationale for invasion, tyranny, and conquest over the New World.

> "I want to tell you something very clear. Don't worry about American pressure on Israel. We, the Jewish people, control America and the Americans know it."
> **- Israeli Prime Minister Ariel Sharon to Foreign Minister Shimon Peres, October 2001**

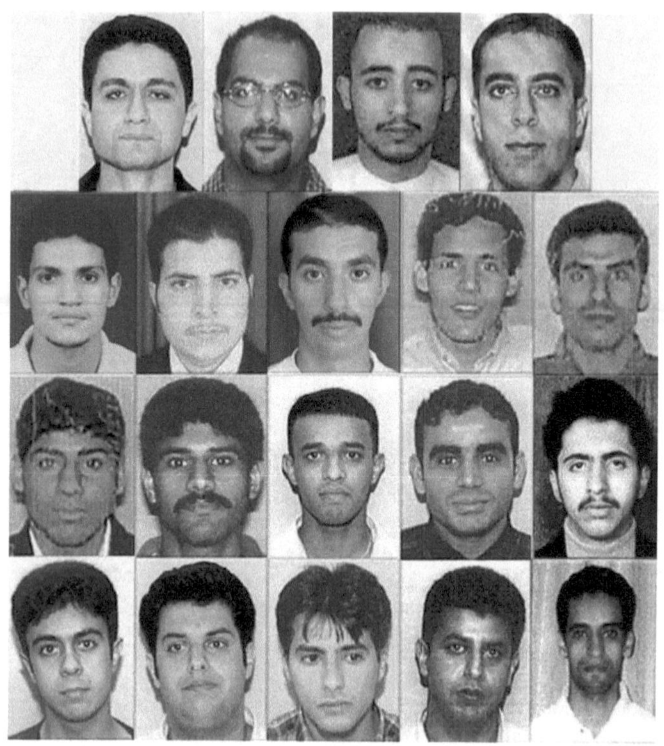

On September 14th, 2001, the Justice Department produced its list with photographs of nineteen men accused of hijacking four separate planes, flights 11, 77, 175, and 93. Over the decades following 9/11, four new names have been added to the list of purported suspects. Another six names have been inexplicably swapped out completely in an attempt to obfuscate the embarrassing lack of evidence produced in subsequent FBI investigations to support claims that these men participated in 911 hijackings. Yet, no eyewitnesses accounts nor video surveillance from any international or domestic airports worldwide have produced any proof that these men even existed. That is until 9 of the 19 identified men have since come forward, outraged that their names and photographs were used accusing them of International Terrorism and to prove that they were still very much alive, not dead in an "airplane suicide bombing."

One of the most damning pieces of evidence for why the Justice Department's supposed investigation into 9/11 is an absolute fabrication comes right out of the 9/11 Commission Report from Robert Bonner, former Senior Director of Drug Enforcement Agency, who stated that he was given the list of 9/11 hijackers the morning of 9/11 at eleven A.M. which was 24 hours ahead of the official list produced by the Pentagon the following day. Caught in the middle of a big lie, Bonner inadvertently spilled the beans on the 9/11 Hoax. American Airlines was also complicit in the 9/11 hoax, never producing evidence of connecting flights 77 and 11. American Airlines refusal to release its flight records or tangible passenger paper ticket stubs meant that the public's only recourse was to refer to the falsified and lackluster

information at the
Department of
**FBI'S ALLEGED
RINGLEADER
AND
MASTERMIND,
"MOHAMED
ATTA," ALSO
FOUND AMONG
THE LIVING**

**AFTER 9/11 IS SEEN IN THE TOP
PHOTOGRAPH AS THE MOSSAD
AGENT WHO DISGUISED HIMSELF
AS A PALESTINIAN 9/11**

TERRORIST (BOTTOM PHOTO).
Justice's website, where only a fabricated diagram of passenger seating could be found.

Among the list of the hijackers who were found still alive after 9/11 was the alleged mastermind behind the operation, Mohamed Atta, who is alive. However, he is the single 9/11 suspect who was, in fact, a MOSSAD agent who was able to disguise himself as a Palestinian Terrorist. This was later discovered when American State-Run Media released a January of 2000 pre-9/11 video in 2008, showing "Mohamed Atta" (whose real name is unknown) with a Zionist friend. D.C.'s Saudi Arabian Embassy reported in "The Independent" that FBI's 9/11 suspect, Abdul Aziz showed up at its Jeddah, Consulate on September 17th, 2001, also outraged after finding his name and picture among the FBI's falsified 9/11 terrorist list. Saeed Algamdi was proven alive in Tunis, appearing in an on-air interview with Asharq Alawsat News. Al-Shehri was also found alive after 911, appearing on Alqods Arabi News. Waleed Al-Shehri was reported amongst the living where he currently works for Saudi Airlines in Morocco, as did Salem_Alhazmi in Saudi Arabia. This was also verified by the Saudi Embassy in Washington D.C. Ahmed_Alnami is also alive, not being involved in 9/11, and is currently employed by Saudi Airlines as Head Supervisor.

While it should now be apparent that 19 "Muslim Terrorists" with "boxcutters" were not involved in the murder of over 3000 Americans or in bringing down the Twin Towers (North and South), or building 7, which appeared to collapse at free-fall speed on September 11th inexplicably. The next logical question to ask now is, who did it?

Several government-made psyops campaigns and theories take the extreme alternative position, placing MOSSAD Agents at the scene of the crime. Yet, this theory has several problems since it is based upon a single photograph showing an "Israeli student" inside one of the Twin Towers (the photograph does not tell us which tower) with what appears to be dynamite in his hands. This photo alone is very enticing to believe since a great many of those involved in the eight trillion-Dollar scam behind the 9/11 conspiracy were very much Zionists; The Bankers, the high-ranking Government Officials, the Media Moguls who ran State-Run propagandized Media, the CEO's and owners of the corporations inside the Twin Towers were all predominantly Zionist and absolutely involved in the World's Greatest American Heist. However, there are two distinct components to the 9/11 conspiracy, the scam and the attack on the World Trade Center itself. Thus, although one could easily mistake the 9/11 conspiracy as being one-dimensional and only involving Israel's MOSSAD, the fact is, the American Government and many other International Governments and its agencies, including MOSSAD, were also complicit in the 9/11 attacks. Furthermore, the attack on all three World Trade Centers were exactly 33 years in the making, from the initial construction of the WTC complex in 1968 to its controlled demolition in 2001, making the in-plain-sightness of 33 not coincidental. This must not be overlooked since the WTC Towers, and its land were Rockefeller owned, with Rockefeller himself being a known high-level Freemason and long-time proponent for the arrival of a complete New World Order.

David Rockefeller further incriminates himself calling for the perfect crisis and fulfillment before the 9/11 crisis took place:

"We are grateful to the Washington Post - New York Times - Time Magazine & other publications who have attended our (Bilderberg) meetings & have honored their discretion for almost fourty years. It would've been impossible to develop our plans for the world if subjected to the bright lights and publicity. But now the world - is more sophisticated - and prepared to march towards a New World Order. The super-natural/ sovereignty of the intellectually elite &

its world bankers are preferable to the nationalistic determination of the past."

– *David Rockefeller's Bilderberg Meeting, 1991*

"This present window of opportunity, during which a truly peaceful and interdependent world order might be built, will not be open for too long. We are on the verge of a global transformation. All we need is the right major crisis and the nations will accept the New World Order."

- David Rockefeller, September 23rd, United Nations Meeting, 1994

Rockefeller further implicates himself in his book, "Memoirs," which was written during September 11th, 2001, then published in 2002 as a final attempt to purge himself from his family's war crimes and crimes against humanity:

"Rockefeller family - for the inordinate influence that they claim which we wield over the American political & its economic institutions. Some (conspiracy-theorists) even believe that we must be part of a secret cabal which works against the best-interests of the United States - characterizing my family and I as 'internationalists' who are conspiring with others ---around the world in building an integrated international political and economic structure--one world Government, if you will. If that's the charge, I stand guilty & I am proud of it." **- David**

Rockefeller, From his autobiography, "Memoirs."

"9-11 was planned - going back to
the early 1970's - if not before. The
World Trade Centre towers were
built already and with 9/11 in
mind, one was David, and the
other Nelson - around the
Rockefeller brothers. I grew up
with these guys. Dick Cheney was
the chief of operations officer for
9/11 conspiracy. I used to go up to
the Rockefeller's estate in Maine
and was on the inside of
<u>Rockefeller's operation, and his
board, which operated as the
upper-theatre of Masons</u>. This is
where they developed the
integration of its front companies -
like SSAIC and the Livermore
labratories to develop the
technology for HAARP [it's Directed
Energy Weapons] which later took

down the World Trade Center Towers."

- **Alfred Webre (Rockefeller Associate during the construction of the WTC Towers), 2008**

Here, Webre suggests HAARP and its Rockefeller creation of international weather modification technology as the primary source of energy used to knock down the World Trade Center buildings. The principle behind Rockefeller's diabolically inspired HAARP technology is its use of incredibly high-powered and focused radio, electromagnetic, and microwave energy beams, now commonly known as Directed Energy Weapons or "DEW's." These DEW's have been confirmed by the U.S.

military as being the most advanced technology the world has ever known, designed for use in military operations, with the ability to vaporize targets at ranges as far as 3000 miles away.

President George W Bush bows before Pope Benedict XVI

Although the implementation of these Directed Energy Weapons are said to be currently in the production phase and will not be seen until the late 2020s, they have already been used routinely in black-ops operations for decades for "climate-change" induced "wildfires" in California and most notably on 9/11 for the vaporization and microwaved implosion of the Twin Towers.

THE MEDIA

The fools who reject conspiracy inside Government and Industry always ask the same question, "how could so many be involved in conspiracies like 9/11 never come forward to expose it?" Two things are wrong with this question. First, many have come forward, including eyewitnesses, those who survived 9/11, first responders, including firefighters and police, but are simply ignored by a Mass Media, owned outright by World Government. Secondly, within Media, most know what they're getting into with the business of propaganda. Many come right out of secret societies and often the CIA itself, where these Government conspiracies are planned. Most within Media are untalented and scripted degenerates who justify how the game is played with the notion that if they didn't participate in it, someone else would. This applies to both the liberal wing of American Political Mass Media as well as its right-wing. 9/11 is an excellent example of this, with both CNN and Fox News – and its lesser subsidiary News Media brethren being complicit and actively participating in every step of the 9/11 hoax.

CNN was tasked with the job of obtaining the superimposed Computer-Generated Imaging (CGI) of "terrorist-operated planes" from the CIA and then propagating this unforgettable and phony imagery to the masses. There is only one known purportedly self-made video, known as the "Zeckarny footage," which showed what looks like a fairly convincing shot of a plane crashing into the North Tower with a simultaneous explosion. This was supposed to be from an Independent "man of the public." However, Zekarny, who was later found out to be a CGI technocrat for the CIA. There was only one major problem with this CGI footage. It appeared to be shoddily done because it clearly shows the left wing of the CGI aircraft disappearing under an adjacent building just before crashing seamlessly into the Twin Tower. The public noticed, and the original footage from CNN can still be found on the internet, although it has been buried under a mountain of 9/11 propaganda.

Fox News did the real dirty work, being assigned the task of having a cameraman inside of a helicopter a mile or so away, who had the shot of the Twin Towers ready for the first explosion to take place. At this distance, with a zoomed-in image and being in a news chopper, keeping the camera still proved to be a bit challenging since the cameraman (who had a line going vertically down his screen for a split-screen shot of the real explosion at the North Tower and a second shot of the CGI planes appearing to make the explosion. There was also a problem with this scheme, the cameraman jumped a hair as the explosion took place, and the effect of this jolt gave the world the unbelievable image of the nose cone of a CGI "terrorist airplane" popping out of the other side of the steel-reinforced World Trade Tower. If the ability for a lightweight aluminum plane crashing into and then taking down a solid-standing steel-reinforced skyscraper wasn't hard enough to digest, the imagery of a plane slicing straight through the building, only to come out of the other side unscathed was the ultimate mockery for the masses.

WHY DOES 9/11'S GROUND ZERO LOOK LIKE A NUCLEAR EVENT?

9/11's ground zero, or the rubble left from the aftermath of 911, look very similar - to what you would expect to see after an Atomic explosion, with traces of Uranium, fissioned Plutonium, along with Radioactive Isotopes of Zinc, Strontium, and Barium, which can only be found as the result of either a nuclear, thermonuclear, "mini-nuclear," a fission-based explosion, Directed Energy Weapons or a combination of all of the above. 9 percent of Barium has been found at ground zero. 8 percent of Uranium, 9 percent of Plutonium have all been found in trace amounts by the tons have been substantiated, yet remain unexplained by the scientific experts in media, who refuse to admit its existence to the public.

"Yes, I know the Chief 9/11 Organizer (David Rockefeller) personally. Also, before 9/11 - I was so very close to David, that I was the only person who was invited to breakfast with him in Bangkok, on Sept. 12th 2001. In the US - it was 9/11 – and to celebrate the 9/11 event, we drank wine together from his personal collection…but I did not know that before about the nuclear

device under the UN building, but it sounds reasonable to me. Because Controlled Demolition Inc. has patented a technique which used Nuclear Weapons for future demolition, but it sounds reasonable to me."

- **Dimitri Khalezov**

During the construction of David Rockefeller's Twin Towers, two thermo-nuclear reactors were each separately installed in the basements of both the North and South Twin Towers. David and Nelson Rockefeller planned the pre-staged and first Fission-induced Thermonuclear demolition of the World Trade Centers Towers and Building 7 - 33 years in advance, set to be detonated on September 11th, 2001 – this date was chosen since it is believed by the Vatican, in accordance with its Gregorian Calendar, to be the birthdate of Jesus Christ. Rockefeller and his Jesuit Order used this important religious date as a pagan-inspired ritualistic event to signify how they would bring about its complete New World Order, one free from Christianity within the decades to follow.

DIRECTED ENERGY WEAPONS USED FROM THE SKY

On September 10th through 9/11, a hurricane bigger than Katrina swept through Manhattan, one which, if not for the planned detonation of the Twin Towers, would have surely made headlines throughout National State-Run Media. Instead, the scope of Hurricane Erin as seen in the photograph below was triggered by the vast amounts of energy produced by HAARP and its Directed Energy Weapons used on Sept. 11th, used as the finishing touches from the sky which provided the extra "energy" needed to bring the Twin Towers tumbling down to the ground.

9/11's UNREPORTED HURRICANE ERIN SEEN FROM

SATELLITE IMAGERY WAS EDITED OUT BY MASS MEDIA

The Thermonuclear-Fission Bombs installed by the Rockefellers were detonated first from the ground, then the Directed Energy Weapons were engaged from above. The incredible amount of energy produced from these D.E.W.'s created a phenomenon known as the "Hutchinson Effect," coined after the strange and unintended effects found in Directed Energy experiments conducted by John Hutchinson, which Dr. Judy Wood later replicated. The unintentional side effects that occur with Directed Energy include the permanent infusing of unrelated matter similar to those found during the Manhattan Project, the vaporization of matter, weather modification, bending of steel and metal without heat, and levitation and effortless movement of heavy objects. One such strange effect produced by Directed Energy Weapons was seen on September 11th, where Hurricane Erin was formed along the east coast and seemed to gravitate directly towards the World Trade Center. Strangely enough, not only was Hurricane Erin deliberately overlooked by the Media before and after 9/11 but it was also heavily edited and even erased from satellite imagery completely. Extensive investigations and documentation of the strange molecular and sub-atomic disturbances caused by the Directed Energy used to bring down the Twin Towers have since been conducted by Alfred Webre, Dr. Judy Wood, and former Rockefeller associates confirming the use of HAARP and Directed Energy Weapons on 9/11.

Incidentally, the "plane hole" found on the South Tower was also formed using Directed Energy, creating an intense explosion, which can be found in unedited footage from news-choppers and the ground, only showing an explosion with no planes visible in the sky.

THE 9/11 BALL

The 9/11 Ball is seldom if ever mentioned anywhere within the 9/11 truther movement (perhaps, in part because the truther movement itself may be controlled), yet it holds the visual evidence unintentionally caught on live television proving that this 9/11 ball made the South Tower explosion and with the absence of any planes in the sky. Suppose you have followed the 911 conspiracy closely and have never heard of the

9/11 ball. In that case, it may be because the NBC videos and similar footage of various angles of the ball have been heavily scrubbed and buried from the internet, but thankfully can still be found archived at "archive.org/details/nbc200109110831-0912". The following pages are pictures of this 9/11 Ball, which have been estimated to be metallic, oval-shaped, moving at approximately 600 miles an hour, and at a steep 45-degree angle - heading directly towards the spot where the South Tower explosion takes place, creating the gigantic airplane-shaped hole. Suppose you can find the video of the live NBC broadcast on 9/11. In that case, you will find that as the ball approaches the South Tower, moving behind the North Tower, the network cleverly switches to the previous footage of the North Tower to hide the ball and the fact that there are absolutely no aircraft of any kind found in the video. Then the network quickly cues up its "missed shot," which then broadcasts oversized Computer-Generated Imaged airplanes appearing to first "rewind" before crashing effortlessly into the South Tower.

As discussed before, HAARP and its advanced Directed Energy Weapon technology were used for the destruction of both World Trade Center Towers. However, the full effects of the Hutchinson Effect when using these high-powered frequencies and energy fields are not fully known, being held in secrecy. Yet substantial evidence has been documented, filmed, and witnessed by Dr. Judy Wood and John Hutchinson, which show a sort of magnetic force which is also produced with Energy Weapons, similar to the effects seen during the path of the 9/11 Ball, as it is attracted directly towards the South Tower. The inexplicable nature of the movement of the 9/11 ball and the totality of strange events that surround the 9/11 hoax, whether electromagnetically induced or otherwise, merit a more unconventional approach to the way we view outdated and often disproven traditional Einstein-based and Newtonian Physics.

"The day science begins to study non physical phenomena, it will make more progress in a decade - than in all previous centuries of its existence."
— **Nikola Tesla**

CHAPTER 2

THE AMERICAN REVOLUTION HOAX

'Its not against the Americans of the South, alone I am fighting. It is againt the Pope of Rome - his perfedious Jesuits, and its blind & bloodthirsty slaves than agains' the American Protestants which we must defend ourselves. Here is the danger of this position. Rome wants to rule & denegrade the North, as it has ruled and denegraded the South. There are only few Southern leaders who are more or less influenced by these Jesuits. The fact is that the majority of

*Roman Catholics, bishops, preists &
laymen are rebels at heart when they
should not be - in fact, with very few
exceptions - every priest - every true
Roman Catholic should be determined
as an enemy of Liberty."*

**- President Abraham Lincoln
August 1861**

The American Civil War was not at all
a hoax. Still, it was indeed a massive
Government cover-up of the truth
behind why the North & South were
fighting and who were the real
shadow armies pulling the strings for
the Union and Confederate Armies.
The history books still state,
unequivocally, that America's Civil
War was over slavery, taxes, and
fundamental disagreements over
Constitutional and Natural Law when
it was, in fact, a religious war and
America's first Revolution. America's

Independence was not established on July 4th, 1776. America officially became a sovereign Country, Independent from "The Church" on April 9th, 1865.

Why did Abraham Lincoln believe he was fighting the Pope in Rome and his perfidious Jesuits and not the American Confederate Army, even one hundred years after the so-called American Revolutionary War was decidedly won by the American people? What may seem like an extremely odd statement from one of Americas most beloved Presidents, Lincoln was then discussing a subject which any American President has not publicly spoken of before or since that time; Which is the constant warring between the Jesuit Order and Illuminati's Shadow Armies - and the Shadow Wars which have privately taken place throughout American history between these two Secret Societies. While Lincoln was clearly not a member of the Jesuit Order - fighting them brutally through a bloody Civil War - he was a high-ranking member of the Order of the Illuminati. Lincoln did not behave or speak like one who put his elitist secret societal rank above the people's freedoms. Lincoln was also acutely aware of the British stranglehold over the American people and its economy since the hoaxed American Revolution, with their foreign-owned Banks subverting American industry and American freedom. Without an American-owned Banking System in place, America's Bill of Rights and Constitution were nothing more than paper with meaningless inalienable rights written upon them. On March 10th, 1862, Lincoln dissolved the

U.S. Treasury, and used a new American currency backed by Gold, the Greenback, putting American money back into American hands while adding real value to the paper fiat European currency.

While history may provide the illusion of Lincoln being assassinated over his abolition of slavery. 'Honest Abe' was shot and killed in 1865 for his abolition and freeing of the American Banking Institutions from foreign control by the Jesuit Order in Rome and its controlled opposition, the Order of the Illuminati.

"Of course- we know that these radical students are not going to take-over government. What they're going to do is provide an excuse for government to take-over people by

passing more & more repressive laws to keep things under control.'"

- **Frank Capell, New Dawn Magazine – June 1996**

British and American historians' greatest barrier is not attempting to sift through endless historical documents and wartime propaganda to find truth. But in understanding the forbidden and unspoken backstory between American and British Governments and their respective Shadow Governments; the Shadow Armies of the Illuminati and Jesuit Order. Since well-meaning Historians refuse to acknowledge the existence of conspiracy theories within Government, they will never be able to provide accurate accounts of history or its so-called "Revolutions." Accurate American and British Historians will always be full-fledged Conspiracy Theorists.

> *"No, I ought not [publish the book I've written revealing the details in how the American Revolution was hoaxed] for I should* **contradict** *all the histories of the great events of* **the Revolution**. *Let the world admire* **the supposed wisdom and valor** *of our great men.* **I shall not undeceive future generations.***"*
>
> **- Charles Thomson**

The most important takeaway you get from this should be the above quote by Charles Thomson (as recorded by Benjamin Rush and written in "Rulers of Evil" by Tupper Saussy), "Founding Father" and Secretary of the Continental Congress, admitting the American Revolution and its American Revolutionary War were hoaxed deceptions for Americans who lived during the late 1770s and for "future generations."

American and British Revolutions had undeniable parallels involving a State-Run propagandized Media (which attempted to create a manufactured public rebellion), a societal opposition to 'Church and State,' a 'Nation in Crisis,' and an underlying theme of religious wars for religious freedom from tyranny, a "Democratic" Constitution and Bill of Rights; but how much of this pronounced freedom from a "Government Church" have we actually gained, or is it entirely possible that both British and American Revolutions were simply given to us as illusions for what we wanted to hear and what the public was demanding?

While there is much conflicting and varying information about who controls this World and its World Government, most of this is deliberate misinformation. Studies have shown that most recognize a conspiratorial entity proactively working towards some Organization hell-bent on world domination and complete tyranny over the peoples of the world. The confusion begins when the public is asked to name exactly who this group is; the most common answers to who this Shadow

Governing Group is, range from the CIA, FBI, MOSSAD, Freemasonry, The Committee of 300, Knights of Malta, Trilateral Commission, Bilderberger Group, Rothschilds, Rockefellers, to the Illuminati and even a Shadow Chinese Government. The truth is, while the World Order is built up of many smaller and subordinate groups, each with its very own controlled opposition counterparts, this is essentially crafted as just another way to confuse citizens. Complete control over this world only comes from one group. This group has been deliberately divided in two; The Jesuit Order and its manufactured and controlled opposition group, the Order of the Illuminati.

The Roman Catholic Jesuit, or "Jesus Order," was originally crafted by

Government to stifle, control, and dominate pure and absolute Christianity, which it was able to successfully do until society began having its own thoughts about what it meant to be a Christian, becoming wise to the Anti-Christian hypocrisy of the institutionalized religion of the Roman Catholic Church. So, what does the most powerful group do when faced with the impossible task of controlling individual minds? Having access - to all of the world's information and hidden knowledge, the Jesuit Order quickly realized the psychology of mind control by force is vastly more complicated. In the end, it was a lost cause if they were to maintain control over the World. So, the Jesuit Order created the Freemasonic and Order of the Illuminati, one after another, systematically taking control over the other half of the World. By giving

American pilgrims what they wanted in search of religious freedom, they also usurped these pilgrims' newly formed religious ideologies with Catholic-controlled opposition Churches. All of their new and burgeoning Churches were, unbeknownst to its congregations, run and owned by the Catholic Church - with the help of the Illuminati. The goal? To destroy pure and absolute Christianity. Christians and every truth would only form as a result of a true and un-meddled-with religious freedom. Any American religious independence from the Jesuits was short-lived. Religious freedoms were only found during America's Colonial period, as the Jesuit-controlled Illuminati and American Government were being established simultaneously on May 1st through July 4th, 1776. The perfect union between the Illuminati and Jesuit Order was established in America to complete a New World Order, one united in a Luciferian tradition. The founding fathers were not advocates for religious freedom. They were agents for the Jesuit Order and advocates for an enhanced Anti-Christian World built upon deception and a Hoaxed New World.

In this way, all Centralized Intelligence in the United States began with George Washington. The foundational building blocks for shaping the eventuality of a widespread and prevailing world-societal ignorance from all truth had been established. This centralized control over all beliefs, big or small, Christian or Judean, were to be governed within these rapidly forming and Shadow-Controlled so-called 'Anti-Catholic' Churches.

Thus, the founding fathers and the British Government deemed it necessary to shape American society and its New World with a hoaxed reality for the dumbing down of its citizens and absolute control over the masses.

"The trilateral commission is global and intended to be the vehicle for multi-national consolidation of the commercial & banking-interests in seizing control of the politics of government of the United States. The Trilateral Commision comprises a skillful and co-ordinated effort in which to seize control over the four centers of power - political, intellectual, monetary & <u>ecclesiastical</u>."

—Barry Goldwater on the role of World Government in seizing power over Christianity

While it's true, the CIA was later established by President Roosevelt in 1947, the Office of Strategic Services (S.S) was already in place in 1945, and George Washington secretly created his very own Centralized Intelligence long before these front groups were in place. Washington did it with the help of his lifelong friend, Nathan Hale, founder of Yale University, later becoming Washington's first 'Chief of Intelligence.'

"We will know our disinformation program is complete when everything the

American public believes is false."

- *CIA Director, William Casey, 1981*

Discovering this sort of disillusionment in Governments' conspiracy against the people, since its inception, may be a tough pill for some Americans, who were raised on the predominant belief that the founding fathers were Pro-Christianity. Yet, let there be no doubt about it, the Founding Fathers did not only oppose a Church & State doctrine but opposed any kind of free-thinking Christianity altogether. Thomas Paine was a testament to the fact that the founding fathers were all vehemently Anti-Christian and believed in replacing any existing traces of American Ideology built upon the tenants of Christianity with what Paine called "reason." In his book, "Age of Reason" Paine states:

"What I see throughout the greater portion of this book (in the Bible) scarcely any thing than a history of the grosest vices & a collection of the most contemptable & paltry tales, I can not dishonor my beliefs by calling it by his name. I dont believe in what is professed by the Jewish Temples, or by a Roman Catholics, by Greek Churches, not by the Turkish, nor the Protestant Church, nor by any church that I know of. My own - mind is my church. The lie of Christ, spoken of in the New Testament & the wild - visionary doctrine raised therein, this is which I contend."

The true story behind the hoaxed American Revolutionary War begins with a deeper look at

British Agent and first anointed Jesuit Illuminatus' President, George Washington (sometimes called "The Fox"), also known to other secret agents as agent #711. Washington insisted: "The necessity of procuring good intelligence is apparent and need not be urged any further. All which remains for me to add to the matter is that you keep what happened [of this hoaxed American Revolution] as secret as possible - For with secrecy, success very much depends - in most enterprises, and for lack of it, they are defeated, even when well-planned & promising favorable issue."

- George Washington, on the importance of keeping secrecy

over the hoaxed American Revolution, 1777

All hoaxed History begins with the principle of the psychological effect of a story premised on a deliberate 'Big Lie' – one so big, outlandish, and miraculous that society cannot negotiate fact from fiction. Instead, it allows Government to decide for them. The American Revolution exemplifies this type of Big-Lie storytelling with a tale of Washington's ragtag army of less than 1,700 untrained standby citizens who somehow had the miraculous ability to crush the greatest Imperialist superpower on earth, the British Army. An army with few supplies, little to no weapons, without uniforms, and to add more Big-Lie storytelling to the story, many of them we are told since there was no British-backed banking for Americans to fall back on, were without shoes. Yet, the tall tale remains absolute for many to this very day, two and a half centuries later. The British army, which, even the history books tell us, won nearly every major battle, from Lexington to Concord – yet somehow the British couldn't tolerate winning anymore, and surrendered, signing the Paris Peace Treaty, finally giving America its Independence. The American Revolutionary War and its Revolution was the first American-made Hoax. With it came a long string of similar incredulous hoaxes and a patriotic illusion of stories so unbelievable that they could only be seen as "Biblical." Thomas Paine may have hated God and The Bible but loved hoaxing the world with fictional stories which had the psychological effect of coming right out of the Bible.

Therefore, this effect could only be the work of a God, who was with America, fighting right alongside the minute-men at the ready and Paul Revere, the fictional character who was never proven to have ever existed. Yet, one whom we are still expected to believe in - who made his famous midnight run through the streets of Boston, warning the Colonists - "British are coming!" This is the psychological nature of Biblically inspired hoaxes. They become emblazoned on our hearts and minds because they are just so incredibly fantastic to resist.

"Without the pen of Paine - the sword of Washington would-have been wielded in vain. History is to ascribe the American-Revolution to Thomas Paine." John Adams famously said this about Thomas Paine. Still, this comment from another founding father is very strange indeed since any bloody Revolution is nearly always attributed to the Generals and soldiers who fought in it, not to the propagandist who attempted to sway public sentiment towards an insurrection - an uprising which at least two-thirds of all Colonialists had absolutely no interest in being embroiled in, and Historical articles from the period show that American Colonists were happy with Government as it was and wasn't interested in a war – especially with the British Empire. The American Government could sell the public on just about anything. Still, the American people weren't biting and could see through the propagandized writings of Paine's "Common Sense," many of them also very much indignant over the Anti-Christian tirades found within his propagandized publications.

Paine also had a secret relationship with founding father, Benjamin Franklin, giving him the unofficial role as British/American double agent with a clandestine American Ambassadorship to France, where he regularly made visits with French Illuminists, the Jesuit Order, and British Agents in Paris, Franklin was able to broker secret deals for the conspired reformation of the British Government over America. This new Government would reestablish all of the same tenants of British Common Law, Constitutional Law, and Bill of Rights with similar verbiage taken from Britain's feigned "Glorious Revolution" and its enlightenment thinkers of the day. British Agents and the Shadow Conspirators of

Europe were now able to successfully plan the execution of a hoaxed American Revolution in secret. The British Naval fleet was to dock in Manhattan first, without American resistance. Later a French Fleet would arrive at Rhone Island. Washington's Intelligence agency, the Culper Ring, would broker communication between the British and French Illuminatist and report all activities back to the British Government.

By 1774 the European Illuminati had already been banished from the German Kingdom of Bavaria for conspiring to overthrow the German Government. The failed coup meant an even tighter Jesuit grip over America's New World was critical. This was all accomplished under a reformed government's veil with a new shadow governing entity and title. The Illuminati would serve as the feigned reconstructed Jesuit Order. The American Founding Fathers working as British Agents would serve to disguise themselves as the opposition to the authoritarian British Government, establishing the appearance of a new American Government on July 4th, 1776. Later, the same Illuminatus' would stage the "French Revolution" for May 5th, 1789. Giving the British, American, and French Governments the hoaxed illusion of a newly formed Democratic and free system of Government for the people, free from the menacing power of the Roman Catholic Church and its Ruling Class Monarchy.

The dates history gives for signing the Constitution, Bill of Rights, and the assignment of Washington's Culper Ring have all been intentionally and deliberately set and coded to happen on very specific dates for those "in-the-know" to decode. These dates also served the purpose of creating confusion and complexity to what amounts to many nonexistent hoaxed events. Notwithstanding, Washington's Culper Ring was most likely set sometime around 1776 and was not a "spy ring," as the founding fathers would have us believe. The Culper Ring were essentially double agents working for British, American, and French Governments.

Washington's Central Intelligence Agency was formed using three of Washington's fellow childhood classmates, three of which were graduates of Yale's University, which is now notoriously known as the birthplace of the brotherhood for 'spooks inside Government' and the formation of the secret society, Skull and Bones. Nathan Hale. Hale volunteered for membership into Washington's Culper Ring but was said to have been suspected of treason by the British and hung from a tree, this account of America's first treason is questionable since Nathan Hale was obviously most identifiable as someone who would be suspected as a spy, and therefore is likely nothing more than more added fiction for a non-event hoaxed Revolution. Nevertheless, Hale was replaced by Major Benjamin Tallmadge and assigned the secret agent_number #721 and his new British Agent name, John Bolton. George Washington, agent #711, British headquarters were #72, and New York City was coded as #727. All of the coded messaging used between British, American, and French double agents were written in the

Culper Rings codebook, giving the Central Intelligence Operators a reference for decoding its private messaging between Agents. America's founding fathers all held a membership in the so-called spy ring and hoaxed networked operation between American, British and French Nations.

The school in which Washington's Episcopal Church childhood friends, Benjamin Tallmadge and Nathan Hale, attended in Setauket, New York, was number assigned 729. Tallmadge then appointed his close friend, Abraham Woodhull, as agent #722, aliased Samuel Culper Senior.

Robert Townsend would become Agent #723. Abraham Woodhull had a tavern in Manhattan's British Headquarters, where Woodhull made social connections that united British and American troops under the newly formed American Government.

Austin Roe (agent #724) relayed top-secret documentation of the developments of the American Hoaxed Revolution back to London, first by horse from Manhattan to Setauket, Long Island. There, agent 725, Caleb Brewster, then delivered these sensitive documents over Long Island Sound using a small ferry boat to Washington's Chief Director of Intelligence, Major Tallmadge in Connecticut, where Tallmadge hand-delivered the Intel back to the "Fox" George Washington, who had its contents sailed across the Atlantic to London.

The Carleton Papers of 1772-1784 have documented undeniable evidence of at least 5000 known

British troops who were paid to desert their command and join the newly formed American, British, and French Aligned Government.

Haym Salomon is mentioned in the Carlton Papers and its military documentation as being British-born and making payments to defecting British Troops listed as employees of the American Government between 1778 and 1783. Others mentioned as employers and extortionists working on behalf of the British Government under Haym Salomon, also later found to be the true creator of the Great American Seal, which can now be found at the back of the one-dollar bill with New World Order subscripted in Latin, also employed more subcontracting British Bankers who assisted in the financing of British Troops these underground extortion rings were James Rivington,

Jonas Hawkins, Mary Underhill, Amos Underhill, Nathaniel Ruggles, Zachariah Hawkins, Hugh Mulligan, A.K.A., "Cato," John Cork, Daniel Bissel, Lewis Costigin and Joshua Davis.

The French Naval fleet arrived at the shores of Rhode Island at the command of General Jean-Baptiste Donatien in 1780. It incredibly was met with absolutely no opposition from the British Navy, utterly surrendering to the French officially with the signing of the Paris Peace Treaty.

America's first great hoaxed event conspired against the American people using a permanent false narrative of an American Revolution fought and won by a small American Militia over the British Empire, forming a new form of Government, free from British and Jesuit influence was a success. Unfortunately, however, the clues for discovering the truth behind this great American hoax were, as are the hoaxed events found today, left in plain sight for those who have eyes to see.

"No, I ought not [publish the book I've written revealing the details in the hoaxed American Revolution], for I would contradict all the histories of the great events of the Revolution - Let the world admire the supposed wisdom & valor of our great men. I shall not un-deceive future generations."

- Charles Thomson, Secretary of the Continental Congress 1774 – 1789

CHAPTER THREE

MOON LANDING HOAX

A complete exploration into American Hoaxism, with its countless American-made hoaxes, made for the development of an ignorant New World Society, would be remiss without citing the Apollo 11 Moon landing hoax. Certainly, the hoaxed mission to the moon ranks among the top five greatest illusions perpetuated by America's World Government. Some may still believe the promulgated lie that there was a "space race" between the United States and the former Soviet Union to establish technological superiority in becoming the first to claim moon territory when technology had nothing to do with it. However, the hoaxed moon landing proved that America was far better at lying to the public and had plenty of experience creating hoaxed realities than the Soviets.

Exactly why the United States felt it necessary to hoax its moon landings is substantially more important than how, simply because it begs the question which the world at large has been wondering for over fifty years, "Why has nobody been to the moon in such a long time?", the little girl asks NASA Astronaut, Buzz Aldrin during the National Book Festival in 2015, to which Buzz replies, "That's not an eight-year-old's question, that's my question, I wanna know, but I think I know: Because we didn't go there, and that's the way it happened." For many, this statement will be the icing on the cake for those who have noticed the mounting implausibility's in the Apollo 11 moon landing and of other "moon landings."

Also, in past decades' similar moon landings, all have been hoaxed, beg an even bigger question, 'why was it necessary to hoax any moon landings at all?' And, since it was necessary, does this mean it is even possible to go to the moon or even space, for that matter? If given the opportunity to ask any one single credible person for this answer, we should insist on asking the father of space exploration himself, NASA's very own founding father, Wernher Von Braun. Yet, since Braun is now deceased, the only place where one can find the answer as to whether or not moon landings or space exploration is even possible now resides at Von Braun's gravestone; where we find engraved, just below his name and time on earth, "Psalms 19:1".

Why on earth would Psalms 19:1 be engraved on NASA's Founder and Director of Space Flight –- the Bible verse which states: "The heavens declare the glory of God; and the firmament sheweth his handiwork."

Psalms 19:1 declares that the heavens or "space" are God's domain, which has a firmament or barrier that cannot be penetrated nor explored. There are two schools-of-thought on the reasons for the apparent impossibility to reach space given by Von Braun. The first school of thought is the watered-down version given by NASA. The barrier ascribed to Von Braun's deathbed-like confession can be ascribed to the deadly and impenetrable radiation belts known as the Van Allen Belts. NASA's Engineer and spokesman, Kelly Smith, admits, "As we get further away from earth, we'll pass through the Van Allen Belts, an area of dangerous radiation. Naturally, we have to pass this danger zone twice, once up and back." Interesting, when speaking about a future exploration into space – while ignoring that, we have been told that manned missions, like the 1969 Apollo 11 moon landing and Apollo 12, as though they never happened.

According to Van Allen himself, the "dangerous radiation" from these Van Allen Belts begins at just 400 miles above the Earth's surface and contains radiation that would "melt human DNA." These radiation belts are said to extend 36,000 miles from Earth, making a manned mission to the moon an impossibility.

"The plan that NASA has is to build a rocket called SLS, which is a heavy-lift rocket – it is something which is much bigger than we have today – and it will be able to carry humans onboard. **Right now, we can only fly inside Earth's orbit (less than 1000 miles above the earth); that's as far as we can go.** And the new system will allow NASA go **beyond and hopefully take humans out of Earth's orbit,** to explore – **the Moon, Mars, Asteroids.**"

– ISS Commander, Terry Virts

The second school of thought for Braun's admission for an inability to reach space has been attributed to the existence of a literal firmament, which is not NASA's version, but instead the Biblical account of a very literal barrier, which encloses every one of us under a solid and dome-shaped structure. This Firmament is believed to be approximately 1000 miles above the Earth (strangely similar to the height of NASA's Van Allen Belts) and is made of a substance as clear as glass and impossible to penetrate. Whether or not you believe in a Domed Firmament or Van Allen Belt barrier, the key to the elusive question for why we have been unable to reach the moon or "space" can be found upon Von Braun's gravestone is the same in both cases; that is, there is a very real barrier which prevents us from reaching the heavens, making space exploration and all its moon landings just another fairy-tale found within the annuls of American Hoaxism.

In addition to NASA's implicit admission to its inability to enter space, inconsistencies found in Apollo's supposed manned moon landing footage reveal what can only be characterized as a blatant mockery of the intelligence of the American people. One of the most unbelievable claims is that in 1969, President Nixon communicated live via radio transmission with astronauts, which were 238 thousand miles away; when the furthest radio transmission recorded in history is only 10,853 miles, set in 2001. This record stands in the

Guinness Book of World Records as the furthest transmission recorded via radio signal. Yet, there is still no mention of Nixon's radioed phone call to the moon in 1969 in any record books, which would have devastated the 2001 record, a whopping 237,000 miles from Earth to the Moon! NASA's open admission that radio transmission is impossible due to the radioactive disruption caused by its "Van Allen Belts" aside, the ridiculously small and lightweight transmitter used by Apollo 11 astronauts further proves that any communication from Earth to Moon is a complete farce. Prominent Radio and Communications Design Engineers, such as David Vye, have pointed out that without the use of repeaters or high-powered amplifiers in space or upon the moon, which were not in existence in 1969, radio transmission from the Earth to the Moon is an impossibility.

Furthermore, discrepancies between the gravity on the moon and what was presented to the world via Television suggest that all recorded moon landing footage could have only been recorded right here on Earth. Science has never waivered about its conclusion that the Moon's gravity is 1.63 m/s squared, which is approximately 1/6th of gravity found on Earth. It has also been maintained that objects on the moon are able to rise six times higher than on Earth, with six times the accelerated force, yet the only athletic maneuver seen on any supposed moon landings were of cosmonaut John Jung, who was only able to jump one foot off into the air, quickly landing back down - without any apparent acceleration or lift. While its true Apollo 11 space suits weighed 185 pounds, and the average Astronaut weighed about 185 pounds, the combined weight of both an astronaut and spacesuit would have only weighed 61 pounds on the moon. Sixty-one pounds on the surface of the moon would mean Cosmonauts like John Jung would be able to perform spectacular leaps into the air, reaching heights of at least 6 feet into the air with very little effort. Yet, no such feats have been found in any of the televised hoaxed moon landings.

More evidence for hoaxed Apollo moon landings can be found in Stanley Kubrick's cinematographic productions and his partnerships with NASA and the United States

Military. The production of "2001: A Space Odyssey" and the propagandized footage of the first moon landing were simultaneously filmed over four years between 1964 and 1968; both films budgets amounted to a staggering and record-setting 350 million dollars, which was paid directly to Kubrick by the U.S. Government. Some say Kubrick made a deal with the devil when signing NASA's contract for the staged production of all Apollo moon landings, which gave him a limitless bankroll and free slate to produce whichever movies he liked, unrestricted by any form of Government oversight. Although Kubrick previously sought help from the U.S. Military for his production of "Dr. Strangelove," there is no reason to believe Kubrick wanted anything to do with the filming of faked moon landings, in fact, all of Kubrick's movies have left clues indicating a deliberate faking and hoaxed production of the Apollo moon landings, and that he was somehow coerced into making the moon landings appear as real as possible, even with the limitations in cinematic 'special effects' available to him through 1964 – 1968.

"A 2001 Space Odyssey's" credits were originally found naming NASA, the U.S. military, and a long list of all of the space aeronautical corporations among those assisting in the production of the blockbuster 1968 film. As these credits were later whitewashed from the film, Kubrick continued leaving clues in his subsequent movies. Steven King's book, "The Shining," directed by

Kubrick, was one such movie. In Kubrick's version, King's forbidden room 217 was changed to room 237, indicating the hoaxed production of the moon landing and the nature of Kubrick's contractual agreement, vowing silence and non-disclosure in his participation in the filming of hoaxed moon landings, with the distance from the Earth to the Moon is – 237,000 Miles; also the closeup on Jack Torrance's Nazi German-made typewriter, the "Adler," indicating America's behind-the-scenes creation of Nazi Germany; again, when the narrator of The Shining says "Danny had - no idea about the world – and now, he knows – he is no longer a dope about things." as Danny stares at a picture of the Dwarf, Dopey, indicating a sudden awareness of previously unknown propagandized and distorted perceptions of the world, which we are taught we must trust to believe as fools. Kubrick must have seen something in himself in the character Jack Torrance played by Jack Nicholson since Torrance was tricked into a deal with Overlook Hotel's manager, who is seen wearing red, white, and blue (with out-of-context American flags appearing in the scenes shot) having the appearance of being some sort of charming and polished smiling politician. Also worth mentioning is the manuscript found written with the words which appeared to say, "All work & no play makes Jack a dull boy.", was not typed as A-1-1 (ALL), but "A" -"one"- "one" or A-"1"-"1"(A11), indicated that his feigned **A**pollo **11** moon landings may have ruined his career, making his work dull and perhaps driving him crazy in the process.

The moon landings' production offers the most damning clues for the hoaxed cinematography of all Apollo missions to the moon. Many have pointed to inconsistencies found in the production of the moon landings, such as the flag waving where no wind can exist; the fact that an astronaut was filming Apollo 11's landing on the moon before arriving to film it; the way dust settled quickly back to the moon, instead of flying forever through space; and the apparent professional filming ability of the cosmonauts who were not trained in photography and could scarcely see out of their thick and muddied visors. Kubrick filmed Apollo 11, 12, 14, 15,16, and 17

missions partially in the Nevada Desert, and partially at Hollywood's Studios, using something very similar to blue screens,
called Scotch-lite, giving him the ability to have Astronauts, Armstrong, Aldrin, and Collins on-set with a giant Scotch-lite screen, which was stitched together from dozens of smaller Scotch-lite screens.
These Scotch-lite screens were the first so-called 'blue-screens of their kind, and the size of this enormous starless-producing moon-screen was the same as used in the production of "2001, A Space Odyssey". Even for today's standards, the effects are quite incredible, though they presented an array of problems for Kubrick to find creative ways to fix.
First, the grainy quality or granularity of these backdrops made

it impossible to have any lifelike stars in any shots; therefore, they were left with a solid black backdrop- without stars to fill the moon's sky -the production was shoddy-looking from the start - but they'd manage to work around it. The Scotch-lite screens can also be seen, upon careful examination, to show a gap in the clarity of what appeared in front of the screen and from what appeared to lay behind it. Below is just one of many examples found amongst an endless number of similar pictures, all of which have since been recognized by the public; therefore, NASA has stated that all of the film has been recorded over "by accident" and would be unavailable to the public to examine. What's left of Kubrick's hoaxed moon landing footage still provides a mountain of evidence that proves that 'humankind' has never – ever - been to the moon.

CHAPTER FOUR

AMERICAN-MADE COMMUNIST CHINA

In a perfect world, we'd like to believe that our country, the one in which we were born, protects us from and against the intrusion of hostile foreign influence. Unfortunately, however, in the real world, our homelands actively participate with, and in many cases, even go as far as to create the enemies with whom we are later told we must build armies against; Communist China is one such country, which has been completely American-made from the ground up, for the eventual completion of a One-World-Government.

The systematic process by which America created the C.C.P (Chinese

Communist Party) began two centuries earlier in a very similar fashion. The British quietly usurped control over America in the late 1700s, and by the same shadow usurpers, the Jesuit-controlled Illuminati. The Jesuit Order's vision for a 'New World Order' and the establishment of a One-World-Government is over 500 years in the making, being rooted in the idea that America's 'New World' would be the 'Beacon on the Shining Hill' for which the rest of the world would emulate with similar Constitutions and Representative Governments forming a veiled and temporary Western Democracy. These freedoms would then slowly and imperceptibly erode over a period of 250 years, as America silently took control over the rest of the world. This was the plan from the beginning of Western Civilization, to entice the remaining Governments of the world with similar freedoms and Industrial/Technological developments to actively participate in, only to bring these apparent Sovereign Governments and its people to their knees upon the complete formation of World Government and its 'New World Order.' China, however, had always been problematic for the elite in conquering. For thousands of years, the Roman Empire, Napoleon, and the Nazis found China unattainable for conquest using traditional warfare. This is why the British decided upon a long-scale 'silent war' – time not being a factor for the Jesuits, who had nothing but time - against China, using Eastern Illuminati Agents to infiltrate the

"Sleeping Giant" over a period of 200 years.

The silent war the British Empire used on China's Qing Dynasty began with The Opium Wars in 1839, ending in 1942 as the Second Opium War ended. The terminology "Opium Wars" is the deliberate misuse of language used by misled Historians to effect imagery of either traditional warfare or some sort of 'Trade War" between China and the British, when in fact, they amounted to what was essentially an infiltration of China's Qing Dynasty by the British's use of its Chinese double-agents, known as "Triads" or the "Eastern Illuminati."

These "Triads" were the high-ranking Chinese Freemasons, which were injected into the Chinese population by the British Government as early as the 1600s. These effective British Agents were secretly tasked in the drug-dealing business to hook the Chinese Qing population to Opium by the millions. This process took nearly one hundred years. Giving it away initially, by 1839, China had become a vast wasteland of opiate addicts, who could only purchase its dope via the British Government. The calculated effort to flood the Chinese with British imported dope was a success. The Qing Dynasty was forced to block all trade with the British Empire, knowing it would soon irreversibly wreck its economy and workforce. The British, of course, reacted with a declaration of war, burning Chinese Naval port cities and ravaging China utterly, from 1839 through 1869; whatever was left of the Qing Dynasty was surrendered to Imperialist Britain with the signing of the "Unequal Peace Treaty."

"There really are issues of the construction of a **New World Order**. *That is what this is about - And that is the sort of dialogue the Chinese are generally good at…And so a partnership between us is essential. A conflict between the U.S. & China is going to exhaust us both in tactical exercises - it cannot be conclusive. The New World Order has to satisfy both (the United States and China) otherwise - it will lead to tensions -that will exhaust us both."*

- Henry Kissinger

As China was being devastated and conquered by the Imperialists of America and Great Britain, the Eastern Illuminati's Triads transformed themselves from a comparatively small group of Masons into a silent Army of elitist Corporate Chinese Mafia moguls. This Triad-Mafia makes up some of the world's wealthiest and most powerful tycoons today – they are China's economic backbone, functioning as the vigilante and 'Gestapo-like' police force for the C.C.P. Today, China's Triads primarily work in the annual exportation of 150 tons of heroin and opiates throughout the world, forming the Golden Triangle's (Myanmar, Laos, and Thailand) headquarters for the largest Drug Cartel on Earth.

Although the Triads largely function as China's International Drug Cartel, exporting street and pharmaceutical opiate-based drugs, they also dominate Asia's illicit child-trafficking, prostitution rings, and money laundering operations – all centrally based out of Shanghai.

With the full cooperation of the Communist Chinese Party, the Triads and its International Red-Corporate Mafia are assisted by Governmental go-between agents called 'Dragon Heads.' These Dragon Heads keep the illusion of a legal and upstanding world enterprise being conducted between the C.C.P, Triads, and its illicit Cartels, which operate worldwide, exporting drugs and child prostitutes throughout Asia's Golden Triangle, Australia, Great Britain, Canada, and the United States. Most, if not all of the opiate-based Western Medicine produced by Western Pharmaceutical Companies come directly via China's Dragon Heads and C.C.P.

Out of America's newly established Government formed in China in 1832 also came the formation of Skull & Bones – one of the world's most elusive and powerful secret societies. The formation of Skull and Bones was predicated on the secret corporate alliance between East and West, and the cooperative efforts of the collective Governments of the world for the formation of a One-World-Government; one which would form a New World Order based upon the principles of Free Enterprise for the Elite and a Totalitarian and oppressive Government for its citizens. Some simply call this Red Corporate and Western Capitalist alliance formed between east and west; "The Company." And, in the interest of simplicity, in what can sometimes become very convoluted, the use of "The Company" is very appropriate when used in the context of conceptualizing One-World Government, simply because the New World Order is a World Government which is controlled and manipulated by Global Corporations; The Company.

Joseph Brewda's article entitled, Bush's China policy- "Skull & Bones" further explains this secret world union: "Skull & Bones has been a secret society at Yale made up of fifteen student members annually. In 1832 the secret society was formed by William Russell, whose Cooperation later dominated U.S. and China's opium trade. Eli Yale, who founded Yale, also made his fortune smuggling opium for the British East India company. Skull & Bones then became recruiting grounds where it would preservie the most important families - who also became wealthy being involved in the opium trade. These families - whose sons join the fraternity , include the Tafts , Coffins, Sloanes, Bundys, Whitney's, and Paynes- and are - even now – "America's establishment".

"And the hope that each of us has to build a New World Order."

– Nixon Speech in Peking China, 1972

"He (Mao Zedong) visited Peking and, while there, received his serious introduction to communist theory in Li Ta-Chao's Marxist Study Group. Now, to develop a reputation in socialist circles, he had to find a forum to propel his ideology - At this crucial point -the student Union of Yale-in-China gave Mao the position of editor for its journal. Mao accepted & changed the arrangement of the magazine from criticisms and problems to focusing on "thought reorientation."

–Yale Daily News No. 96, September 1972, Yale Digital Library.

Nixon's 1972 meeting with Mao Zedong and Premier Zhou Enlai for so-called peace talks marked the beginning stages for the complete development of an American-made New World Order. But, unfortunately, Chairman Mao and Nixon are mere figureheads among a cast of characters who work for a larger network of high-ranking company management. With Chairman Mao being a known member of America's Yale-in-China's project since 1921, and both leaders actively participating as employees of Skull & Bones Incorporated, this televised charade effecting these two world leaders as "former enemies," forging an alliance for 'world peace' is the epitome of the utter nonsense found throughout State-Run Media and its long history in promulgating American Hoaxism.

China was completely conquered by the United States long before the Nixon/Mao photo-op, and China is simply a straw-man enemy, working hand-in-hand with American foreign policy for the arrival of a New World Order. Bringing China into the New World Order was a giant step in America's acquisition of territory throughout the world. The Middle East was later taken over by the U.S., using

9/11 as the hoaxed mechanism to achieve complete world dominance. Iraq, Afghanistan, Libya, and even Iran have all now been established as American territory (not Governments 'existing in a vacuum,' as we are told). Iran and North Korea are also used as American strawman 'enemies,' who are, in fact, entirely governed by the *U.S.* The pervasive false belief perpetuated by the Media that there are countries that exist today – outside of America's New World Order – is simply a lie for the uninformed masses of a hoaxed world.

While September 11th, 2001, marked the beginning of America's New World dominance over the rest of the world, March 11th, 2020, marked the completion, with the advent of the 'perfect crisis,' spoken of by Kissinger, Rockefeller, and all known advocates for a New World Order was realized; the Scamdemic World Crisis.

"Today Americans would be outraged if U.N. troops entered Los Angeles to restore order – tomorrow they will be grateful, this is especially true if they were told there was an outside threat from beyond, whether real or promulgated, that threatened our very existence, it is then that all the people of the world will plead with world leaders to deliver them from this evil. The one thing every man fears is the unknown- When presented with this scenario, individual rights will be willingly relinquished for the guarantee of their well being granted to them by World Government." – **Kissinger, Bilderberger Meeting**

"This present window of opportunity, in which a peaceful & independent world order may be built, will not be open for very long. We're on the verge of a global transformation. All that is needed is the right major crises, and the nations will accept the - New World Order."

– David Rockefeller, Bilderberger Meeting, 1994

The world has already recently witnessed this 'world threat' or 'right major crisis' unfold, for which the peoples of the world have pleaded with Government to deliver them from. However, since this first major crisis has a W.E.F. expiration date of March 2025 (discussed in detail in Chapter 6), the next major crisis directly involves China and has absolutely nothing whatsoever to do with a plague.

The International Monetary Fund, World Bank, and the U.S. Federal

Reserve are now predominantly owned by Communist China, which currently possesses 1.5 trillion in U.S. Treasury Bonds. How could China possibly own so much stock in American Currency? Because America sold it to them. Why would the United States sell the majority of its stock in its Dollar to Communist China, and why didn't anyone stop it - after all, we are supposed adversaries?

In 1979 China's Central Bank Chair, Zhao Xiao-Chuan, and David Rockefeller met for the cooperative realignment of the world's economy. This U.S. (Rockefeller) Federal Reserve Bank and Chinese Central Bank merger amounts to Rockefeller's deliberate effort for the global emergence of a One World Currency backed by China's recent implementation of the Gold Standard.

In 1971, Rockefeller's Federal Reserve scheme for a One-World-Currency, known as "The Amero," began when the U.S. Gold Standard was indefinitely suspended, and America's Gold, previously held in Fort Knox, was shipped to China's Central Bank repository. Since the suspension of America's Gold Standard, China's repositories today amount to a staggering one million tons of gold bullion. As a result, China was transformed from 1971 to 2014 from a country without Gold to an Economic Superpower, suddenly outdoing the United States and Europe at a nineteen percent economic growth rate annually. This reversal of a prevailing American-based World Economy shifting suddenly into a Chinese-dominated World Economy is no coincidence. It has since been recently accelerated exponentially since the perfect scamdemic crisis was hatched in 2020.

When the American Gold Standard was suspended in perpetuity in 1971, it wasn't long before the American public began asking the logical question, that since the Gold Standard was suspended, "Could this have something to do with an American shortage of Gold?" So, in 1974 the American public was given a very limited and hoaxed inspection of the Gold Bullion supposedly held at Fort Knox. Senators and Congressmen present for the inspection were only given a brief and superficial tour of one tiny room within Fort Knox's depot and noted that the apparent gold bricks' weight seemed light and could move them about easily. Those watching television also noticed a superficial layer of gold - shoddily painted over fake gold bricks.

The public wasn't impressed, and no further 'transparent' inspections have followed since 1974.

What are the ramifications of the Chinese Government using its currency, the Yuan, which the Chinese Government has said will be backed by Gold shortly (likely to happen between 2025 and 2029)? The impact of such a future event would immediately devastate world economies, which do not have gold-backed currency. Currently, every nation on Earth uses worthless paper fiat money, which is only backed by the strength of its Nations' economic production and the illusion of its inherent value.

With over eight hundred Military bases situated around the world, the United States and its Military Industrial Complex extending unofficially into

Western China, Libya, Syria, Burma, Tibet, Iran, and Sudan; China simply has no chance of winning any militarily fought war with the United States, having only one military base in Djibouti, Africa. However, the elites have always played the game within its world theater in the Freemasonic idea of "Order out of Chaos," meaning that the New World Order will form, in its final stages, rising out of the ashes of a dying and chaotic old world. Unfortunately, amid this scamdemic crisis, our world today is in this final stage, and as China continues to be bolstered into an economic superpower. One which can devalue American currency completely, with its ownership of the U.S. Federal Reserve, the vested interest of 19-Trillion worth of U.S. Treasury Bonds, and the looming forecasts for China becoming the only country in the world with currency backed by gold, rendering the U.S. Dollar absolutely useless is a very real threat for America and the rest of the world.

As long as the Jesuit and Freemasonic Orders continue to overthrow the world and the people within it, with hoaxed crises and scamdemics, requiring injections, world passports, QR-coded tattooing, and RFID chipping – China's Gold-backed digital currency- the "Digital Yuan," will be forced upon the peoples of the world, being embedded on our forearms, as the official one-world-currency used by all Nations. By 2025 the scamdemic expirers and a new crisis begins. The United States and China are pre-staged to put the next great world depopulation agenda in place as the beginning of a hoaxed need for World War Three.

CHAPTER FIVE

AMERICA'S 4TH REICH

"The best way to take control over society and control them completely is in taking a little of its freedom at a time, to erode rights by a thousand tiny & almost imperceptible reductions. In this way - people will not notice these rights & freedoms being removed until the point which these changes cannot be reversed."
 – Adolf Hitler

The Fourth Reich is here, and we are living in it. The Fourth Reich is silent, projecting an image of Democracy and Representative Government – from its silence, it draws its power. Out of its ability to transform itself from Democrat to Republican, from bad to "good guys," it becomes imperceptible. World peace is the weapon used to entice Governments into participation in a New Order which has never been peaceful. Tactical exercises and black operations create hoaxed illusions of instability in the world, where none exists. Cures become weapons for those seeking help from Government crises. Silent wars have replaced open warfare, and within the backwardness of this American-made Fourth Reich are the embedded Nazi Third Reich bureaucrats and their technocratic children.

Every President beginning with George Herbert Walker Bush has either been a Son of a Nazi or related directly to Adolf Hitler, the Fuhrer himself. This includes many Senators, Congressmen, Unelected Bureaucrats, Technocrats, and Political Statesmen. Every U.S. President has been either a Rockefeller or a Rothschild (European and American brothers) and a member of the Order of Cincinnati. Out of this royal bloodline, which trace back to King John, we also find world leaders like Adolf Hitler, grandson of Salomon Meyer Von Rothschild, and Angela Merkel, granddaughter of Adolf Hitler. The elitist and Luciferian bloodline make up 13 Anti-Christian families, Freeman, DuPont, Collins, Astor, Bundy, Kennedy, Li, Onassis, Van Duyn, Reynolds,

Russel, Rockefeller, and Rothschilds. The Bush family has also sprung out from the Luciferian bloodline, being both the sons of Rockefeller's and the sons of Nazi's. And Obama is no exception, being the son of Michael Rockefeller, while also being the great grandson of Nazi Eva Von Braun and Adolf Hitler.

The American-made New World Order officially began in March of 1933, the very same month and year in which both German Nazi Chancellor, Adolf Hitler, and American President Franklin Delano Roosevelt were simultaneously installed into office; Adolf Hitler in Hindenburg, Germany and Roosevelt in

Washington D.C as the U.S. and German founding fathers of the silent 4th Reich.

"In politics, nothing happens by accident - If it happens, you can bet it was planned that way."
- Fourth Reich Founding Father, Franklin D. Roosevelt

Unlike Nazi Germany's 3rd Reich, the silent American 4th Reich is not exclusively Anglo-Saxon. The Fallen Angels who possess the spirits, minds, and bodies of the elite understand nature's limitations, yet continue in their pursuits for a Babylonian One-World Government, in finding ways to ascend back into the heavens - from which they were cast out, speeding up the communication needed between Governments for so-called world peace, progress and advancements in technology, and a homogeneous one race. Hitler's 3rd Reich strategy for a Babylonian-like singular "master race" failed, so a new 4th Reich approach was needed to achieve this singularity. The inclusion of all races could work, but this homogeny of mingling races for one singular race, as it was before the tower of Babel (Babylon), is just too time-consuming for a New World with a deadline of between 2030 – 2050. This is when the idea that there was only one way for the silent 4th Reich to reach singularly, the depopulation agenda.

The 'Depopulation Agenda' began in 1921, with Margaret Sanger's birth control movement, which involved the promulgated hoaxed lie of an overpopulated world with limited food and natural resources. The solution to this proposed crisis was the extermination of unborn children with a proactive push for abortion and the use of contraception. But, of course, the world doesn't lack any natural resources, yet since the elite own and control the world's food supply and resources, they have managed to manipulate the illusion of scarcity for the monopolizing of Industry and to create a rationale for depopulation. You may have tried finding the world's actual population, only to find serious flaws in the various answers found on the internet, which range wildly from 5 to 9 billion – an exact and concrete number can never be found. This is because there are nowhere near 9 billion people on Earth. The Earth's population is less than 3 billion, and when adding up every central town and city throughout the world, you find out the world only has 2.8 billion people and is rapidly shrinking. So, the only crisis the elites face is an under-populated world containing an abundance of food, energy, and natural resources, which is deliberately being mismanaged to gain absolute control over the world's peoples.

1933 also happened to be the year Franklin Delano Roosevelt

appointed his fellow Freemasonic friend (also a member of the CFR and Club of Rome) and Nazi sympathizer William Harriman as New York State Committee Chairman of Employment. William Averell Harriman was among the elite group of World Bankers (U.S. Federal Reserve). These bankers were united in forming one multinational conglomerate of mono-national Central Banks (World Bank & U.S. Federal Reserve). These were the same bankers responsible for financing the Communist Bolshevik Revolution, World War 1, and World War 2. Meeting in secret, President Roosevelt, Adolf Hitler, Nazi Germany's Central Bank Chairman, Hjalmar Schacht, William Harriman, Emil Kirdor,

U.S. Federal Reserve Banking Chairmen; Paul Warburg, Max Warburg (also co-owner of Nazi Germany's I.G. Farben), Walter Teagle; together with the leaders of American Industry: from Thyssen and Company, General Electric, Bayer, Hoechst, Ford, General Motors, BASF, and Nazi Germany's I.G. Farben plotted the economic fueling of the rise of Nazi Germany and advent of World War II. The atrocities, war crimes, and depopulation to be committed were rationalized as the means to an end in the acceleration of a New One-World Economy, one brought about by the deliberate and planned use of World War. Emil Kirdor, who shadow-engineered this meeting for the planning and cooperative alliance for a manufactured World War 2, describes the meeting:

"In 1923, I first came into contact with the National Socialist movement. I first heard the fuehrer in the Essen exhibition Hall - His clear exposition completely convinced & overwhelmed me... in 1927, I first met the Fuehrer personally. I traveled to Munich & there had a conversation with the fuehrer in the Bruckmann home - During four and a half hours, Hitler explained to me his program in detail - I then begged the fuehrer to put together a lecture he had given me as a pamphlet - I then distributed this pamphlet in my name, in business and manufacturing circles. Then I placed myself completely into his

movement - Shortly after our Munich conversation & as a result of the pamphlet the fuehrer composed & I distributed a number of meetings took place between the fuehrer & leading personalities in the field of industry. Before the taking over of power, leaders in industry met in my house together with Hitler, Rudolf Hess, Hermann Goering, & other leading personalities of the party."
- One-World Economic Ringleader, Emil Kirdor

When speaking about the Great Reset, the 4th Reich spokesman, Klaus Schwab, has said, "We are now entering the 4th Industrial Revolution." Well, what on earth does that mean to those of us outside of the Cabal? To Klaus, it simply meant that each Reich (1-4), two World Wars (2nd and 3rd Reich), and Scamdemic (4th Reich) were all fueled by the shadow-masters of Industry and the shadow-armies who manipulate and control society. But, of course, the layman does not understand that every world event has been conspired against the people of the world for the completion of a tyrannical and Luciferian New World Order.

Proof of President Franklin Delano Roosevelt's support for Hitler's New World Order and the rise of Nazi Germany's 3rd Reich go back as far as 1925, when Roosevelt and fellow Nazi Propagandist, Putzi Hanf-staengl, published the "Volkischer Beobachter" or Nazi

Daily Journal in order to condition Germans to conform to Nazi ideology and to prepare them for Hitler's rise to power in 1933. Roosevelt also strongly advocated Socialism for Americans when signing his "New Deal" into law for an American Welfare State. The "New Deal" was identical to Nazi Germany's "Four Year Plan," the only difference being that Nazi Germany lost the war, never allowing its "Four-Year Plan" to take effect. In contrast, Roosevelt's veiled American Socialism is progressively permanent.

Roosevelt's participation in the development of the 3rd Reich's Nazi Germany meant the smuggling of Nazi Germany's Technocratic elite into American Government was a forgone conclusion; This process is otherwise known as Operation Paperclip, wherein at least 2,000 known Nazi war criminals were given immunity and imbedded into Intelligence agencies, set up by F.D.R: The Federal Bureau of Investigation in 1935, the Pentagon on September 11, 1941, and the C.I.A. in 1947.

Finally, in 1933 President Roosevelt dissolved the American Constitution and the United States Government, transforming it into a Global Corporation; U.S.A INC. AMERICA officially declared Bankruptcy as F.D.R instituted the Emergency Powers Act, forcing the United States Constitution into permanent suspension with the annual declaration of National

Emergencies (declared yearly by either by U.S. Presidents or secretly by Congress within unseen Omnibus Bills) and putting the American Government into a perpetual state of Martial Law - Maritime Law.

CHAPTER SIX
3/11

"Agenda 21 proposes a array of actions which intend on being implemented by every person on Earth, effective execution of Agenda 21 requires a profound reorientation of all mankind - unlike anything the world has experienced."
- United Nations, "Agenda 21, from Earth Summit Strategy to Save our Planet", 1991

Most do not realize that the scamdemic world crisis, which the peoples of the world are now attempting to survive, has an expiration date of March 2025 – and this information is available to the public, in plain sight, via the World Economic Forum. This WEF international contract between all nations of the world is pictured below and should offer some needed insight into what is happening beyond what we are programmed to believe; depending on which political party, or State-controlled ideology you have identified with, we'll get a host of intentionally false information designed to distract us from the reality of it all. This scamdemic world contract means this crisis is being managed as a business with a beginning and an end. Take a moment to digest that, and what that means – since we are currently living under the World

Government's Fourth Reich, I can only spell it out for you.

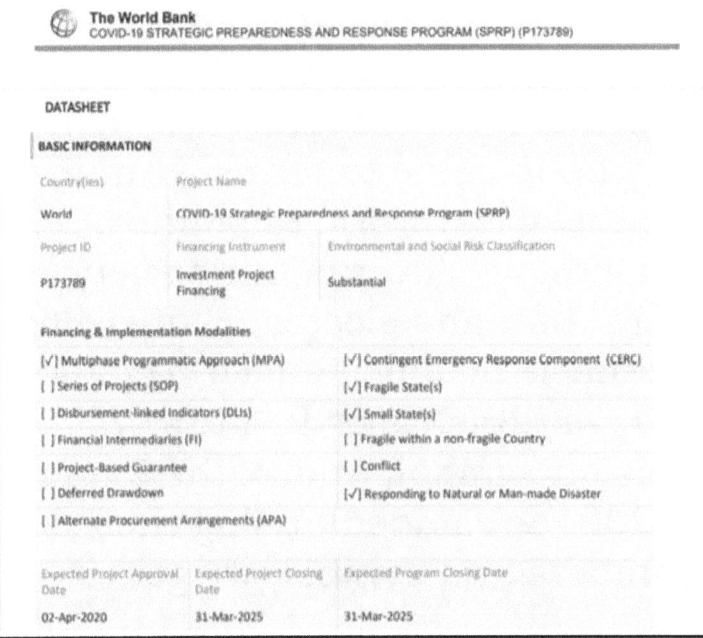

The World Bank
COVID-19 STRATEGIC PREPAREDNESS AND RESPONSE PROGRAM (SPRP) (P173789)

DATASHEET

BASIC INFORMATION

Country(ies)	Project Name	
World	COVID-19 Strategic Preparedness and Response Program (SPRP)	

Project ID	Financing Instrument	Environmental and Social Risk Classification
P173789	Investment Project Financing	Substantial

Financing & Implementation Modalities

[✓] Multiphase Programmatic Approach (MPA)	[✓] Contingent Emergency Response Component (CERC)
[ ] Series of Projects (SOP)	[✓] Fragile State(s)
[ ] Disbursement-linked Indicators (DLIs)	[✓] Small State(s)
[ ] Financial Intermediaries (FI)	[ ] Fragile within a non-fragile Country
[ ] Project-Based Guarantee	[ ] Conflict
[ ] Deferred Drawdown	[✓] Responding to Natural or Man-made Disaster
[ ] Alternate Procurement Arrangements (APA)	

Expected Project Approval Date	Expected Project Closing Date	Expected Program Closing Date
02-Apr-2020	31-Mar-2025	31-Mar-2025

Although this world contract cites April 2nd, 2020 as the beginning, the world crisis began on 3/11/2020, when a National Emergency was declared.

Incidentally, conspiracy realists have been aware of a 9/11-like event to come on 3/11, although many had the circumstances which would surround it and the year indeterminate. As hard as it may be to come to terms with, in the theatrical world of politics, numerology governs our society more than any elected or unelected technocratic official does. The date of 9/11/2001 uses 9, 11, a "/" division symbol, and 3 (the 2 and 1 in 2001 are added); using these numbers and symbol, we get:

$$9 \times 11 = 99/3 = 33$$

Again on 3/11, the date of 3/11/2020 uses 3, 11, 2 and "/";

using these numbers and symbol, we get:

$$3 \times 11 = 33 \times 2 = 66/2 = 33$$

The Freemasonic 33 can clearly be seen on both 9/11 and 3/11, once the Kabalistic numerology is applied. If this isn't enough to convince you - the fact that on both dates, 9/11/2001 and 3/11/2020, official National Emergencies by the President were declared, which suspended the U.S. Constitution, putting the United States under Martial Law.

Since America has laid claim over the Nations within its New World Order, under Martial Law, all countries now exist under the tyranny of World Government. This

Maritime State we now live in has forever restructured the world's governments into one International Corporation.

"A robust economic recession has already begun, and we could be facing the worst depression since the 1930s. However, while this outcome is likely, it is not inevitable. Society has to act together - swiftly to renew all aspects of our societies and economies, from education to social contracts and working conditions. *Every country, from the United States to China, must participate, and every industry, from oil and gas to technology, must be transformed.*"
– Klaus Schwab

Suddenly, and without rational explanation, the Scamdemic has shifted from a medical crisis to a transformation of the World's natural resources and an urgency to prevent climate change. Of course, there is no correlation between epidemics and climate change. However, crises were needed to bring society into "lock step," as David Rockefeller outlined in "Event 201", to initiate Agenda 2030, also known as Agenda 21.

Agenda 21 is the true agenda behind the crisis the world is facing today. It is not a "conspiracy theory" since the United Nations has decreed it as international law, which must completely take effect by 2030. Agenda 2030 also comes out of United Nations International

Law and is the extensive version of Agenda 21; Agenda 21 is code for when these agendas began, 2021. 2030 is the deadline. However, it will be completed in 2029. Since all history has been pre-planned, so too has our future. This is not something prophetic or something theoretical, it is simply a matter of reading the writing on the wall, and if you watch closely, the big picture is clear to see.

Agenda 21 is the world depopulation agenda and the systematic restructuring of all human resources, including human beings, hidden behind the veil of climate change; this global agenda was precipitated by the use of the scamdemic as a tool for the rallying call for an international crisis. Ownership of private property will cease to exist, and all property, resources, and people are to become the property of the State. The middle class, under Agenda 2030, will become eradicated from Earth, leaving only the New World Elite and the poverty-stricken slaves of the State.

*"The only way out from the double-bind of poverty & environmental disruption calls for a long period of economic growth to sustain the transition strategies towards the **virtuous green path** of what has been called in Stockholm **eco-development** and has since changed its name in Anglo-Saxon countries to **sustainable development**. The bolder steps are taken in the near future; the shorter*

will be the time span that separates us from a steady-state. Radical solutions must address the roots of the problem & not to its symptoms. In theory, the transition could be made shorter by measures of redistribution of assets and income."

- United Nations, Jeffrey Sachs "The Next 40 Years: Transition Strategies to the Virtuous Green Path"

Rural Americans are to be evacuated from their homes, by either Military force or force of nature (Directed Energy Weapons), into condensed and populated cities called 'human resettlement zones.' Within these human resettlement zones, rural Americans will be placed into public housing projects retrofitted as smart homes, with meters on all appliances to regulate all food, water, and energy consumption. In addition, climate Action laws will be put into place, which are already laws that will take effect retroactively. All activities will be monitored via sensors and cameras placed throughout these homes and will assess who will be fined or imprisoned for violation of any Climate Action Laws. These Smart Homes within Smart Cities and FEMA camps are already being built in metropolitan cities throughout the United States and the New World - the very first smart city being built in Wuhan, China, which is now being used in accordance with International Law, reducing all household energy and food consumption by eighty percent. The Rockefeller Commission has publicly released its 'Resettlement Zone Map,' shown below, dividing America into eleven zones. World Government intends to seize and take possession of the vast farmland and industrial areas shown in grey. The darker grey zones show areas where these displaced rural and suburban Americans will be migrated like herds of cattle into these policed human resettlement zones, equipped with housing projects, not to exceed 500 square feet of living space.

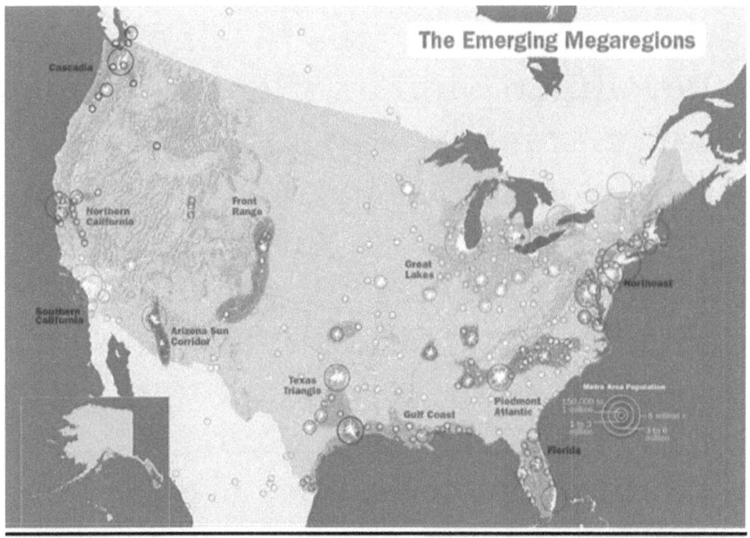

After the scamdemic crisis contract expires in 2025, unfortunately, a new series of crises have been pre-staged to occur between 2025 – 2030. As America continues to Govern China while paradoxically giving them absolute dominance over U.S. and world economies through the W.E.F. scamdemic contract – this contract is set to end in March of 2025. Once this contract is made null and void, dominance over this "4th Industrial Revolution" and its silent weapons can ultimately only be settled in war. Does this mean World War III between East and West? Absolutely, and all the political timelines and Chinese and U.N. agendas point to 2025. Though this World War is set to be relatively swift and decisive, it will involve the use of so-called nuclear weapons and will successfully depopulate the world on a scale we have never seen before. Whistle-blower, Bill Ryan has described this shocking set of planned events with great accuracy as early as 2010: "We received an 11-page document from an insider who attended the Senior Masons Conference in London in 2005. The content of the discussion was really outrageous. Our intelligence provider reports: The Third World War is about to happen. This is already planned. It will be a war of nuclear weapons and biological weapons. Our intelligence sources believe it will begin in the next 18-24 months. The plan starts with Israel's crackdown on Iran. Iran or China will be provoked in response to a nuclear weapon. After a brief nuclear exchange, there will be a ceasefire. The World will be plunged into fear and chaos-all of which are carefully designed. Extreme tensions will be used as an excuse and justification for heavy social and military control in all Western First World countries. Plans are ready in this place. During the nuclear ceasefire, there was a secret release of planned biological weapons. At first, these goals were aimed at the Chinese. Our intelligence providers tell us chillingly, "China will catch a cold." Biological warfare will spread further to the West. Infrastructure will be severely weakened. This is just the beginning of the plan. After this, a full nuclear exchange will be triggered: this real war will cause extensive damage & loss of life. Intelligence tells us that through these plans include the reduction of the population by fifty percent. When I heard the number which was given in the meeting and that this horrific scenario has been in the planning - for generations, I felt terrible. The first II world wars were planned for the doomsday-revelation & the 2008 housing market collapse, which was also very carefully planned to accelerate a centralizing of financial resources. As if all what I heard was not enough, my information provider told me that all of this was calculated to deal with the coming geo-physical event - Similar events before. If this event happens- not necessarily in 2012, but sometime around the next ten years or so - we know that it will destroy all civilization - more than an impact of a nuclear war. I asked my informant: If there was expect to be a disaster - why would you initiate World War III? His answer - made me feel horrible. He explained that the true goal was to create a disaster world after its establishment. To ensure this "new world" that the controllers want - totalitarian control structures it must be in place at the time of this catastrophe-on the pretext that the people must accept & ask for - martial law to be brought about for the cause of justice. These countries that have been carefully scrutinized for selection its for military-operation at which time would allow the right people to survive & prosper in this post-disaster age - it is about nothing more than who ("which right people") will inherit the planet."

In this scenario, the New World Order's "Order out of Chaos" credo would be even more dramatic than we could have ever imagined. Yet, supposing even some of these events, its numbers, and exactly how this depopulation plan is achieved, whether by nuclear war or by some other means of the use of silent weapons designed to kill, the endgame and outcome are the same; depopulation of what is left of the undesirable people of the old world for the rebuilding of a Totalitarian and dystopian New World.

As we have seen, there has never been any Revolution involving any sort of "revolt of the people" anywhere, at any point in world history. Revolts are simply an American-made hoaxed concept giving us a false sense of security from an oppressive Government. Moreover, to place our trust in politics or its savior-like leaders to save us from crises, which they've created, is also equally misguided and ignorant. But, if we cannot help ourselves, then who can? Only God can save us from the Luciferian-led Whore of Babylon. To ask for help from anyone or anything else is pure ignorance.

'For we wrestle not against flesh & blood -- but against principalities, against powers - against the rulers of the darkness of this world - against spiritual wickedness in high places.'
- Ephesians 6:12

"We will know our disinformation program is complete when everything the American public believes is false."
- CIA Director, William J. Casey

Although we do not have direct power over the Babylonian New World Order, we do absolutely have the power of a deeper awareness of its constant and relentless barrage of hoaxed lies and illusions. A complete acceptance that everything we have been taught to believe about politics, science, scientific breakthroughs, technology, the medical community, modern medicine, the universe, space, the mechanics of the earth, history – are all lies – may take time – but without the understanding of American Hoaxism, the world around us becomes a matrix of pitfalls from which there is no escape.

Our American Flag can be seen window-dressed throughout courtrooms within the United

States of America, including the Supreme Court, which is also compromised as an un-politically biased club of elitists. But, unfortunately, this flag which you may have seen in what is supposed to be an American Justice System for the people, is not American at all and does not abide by the tenants of our so-called American Constitution. So instead, what you are witnessing is the Admiralty Flag, which is the flag representing our country under Martial Law. With its golden-laced frilly borders along its edges, it is an open mockery of Justice in a Hoaxed America. Suppose you ever are unfortunate enough to find yourself in one of these Maritime-State courtrooms. In that case, you will soon realize that the justices spoken of in our American Constitution are just words - on a piece of paper, which only have a theoretical value that may be interpreted at the U.S. Supreme Court. Unfortunately for the average citizen, the Supreme Court only takes less than a dozen pre-screened cases a year, so interpretation of a deliberately vague Constitution is not possible.

In any case, what is left of American Sovereignty? Ignorance can be bliss. Sometimes this can be the case, but the truth shall set you free, however difficult it may be initially on our very souls. There is nothing left of America but lingering illusions and hoaxes of what used to be. All of the conspiracies brought about against American and World citizens have been planned from the very beginning. As beautiful as illusions may seem, they are also Government inspired illusions of safety and peace from a Government that does not encourage free thought and is very much set against each one of us— knowing that we can be so easily fooled, programmed, and reprogramed daily - We can also deprogram and reprogram ourselves with our very own illusions and realities about our world, which have the power to become just as real as the hoaxed realities we have come to accept from World Government willingly.

Our minds and souls are under continuous assault. Our duty as free-thinking individuals is to form our own perceptions of the world around us—one outside the totalitarian grip of the hypnotic influence of a progressive and ever-changing American Hoaxism.

9 798751 279424